CYCLE A GOSPEL TEXTS

FROM ANTICIPATION TO TRANSFIGURATION

SERMONS FOR ADVENT,
CHRISTMAS, &
EPIPHANY

JOE E.
PENNEL, JR.

C.S.S. Publishing Co., Inc.

Lima, Ohio

FROM ANTICIPATION TO TRANSFIGURATION

Library of Congress Cataloging-in-Publication Data

Pennel, Joe E.
 From anticipation to transfiguration

  1. Advent sermons. 2. Christmas sermons. 3. Epiphany season — Sermons.
4. Methodist Church — Sermons. 5. United Methodist Church (U.S.) — Sermons.
6. Sermons, American. I. Title.
BV40.P45 1989   252'.61   89-9884
ISBN 1-55673-126-4

9851 / ISBN 1-55673-126-4

To
Thelma and Joe
Deloris and Leonard
for Their steadfast love
and thoughtful example

Table of Contents

Preface

This book contains sermons preached at Belmont United Methodist Church, a mid-city congregation of believers in Nashville, Tennessee. Some of these sermons have been transcribed from a tape recording of Sunday services and have been included in this book with very little editing or polishing. Others are examples of manuscripts written prior to the preaching event but not used during the actual delivery of the sermon. A few were written after the Sunday on which they were offered. Thus, the reader will notice a vast difference in tone and style.

I offer this book with great reservation because preaching is basically and fundamentally an oral process. Reading a sermon does not allow one to hear the various inflections of the human voice. Nor does it permit one to see gestures or facial expressions. Furthermore, reading does not take into account the preacher's personality. Nor does it place the sermon in the larger context of public worship. In spite of these reservations, I have agreed to submit these proclamations to a larger audience with the modest hope that they will help the reader reflect upon life from the vantage point of the themes and meanings expressed during the seasons of Advent, Christmas, and Epiphany.

I have written these sermons for ordinary people, both young and old. It has not been my intention to acquaint the reader with the critical speculations or the linguistic details that interest scholars. I have tried to serve the biscuits but not the recipe. William Tyndale once boasted that he wanted the boy who drove the plough to know more of the Scriptures than did the Bishop of London. The great task for Tyndale was to popularize scriptural study by translating the Scriptures from Hebrew, Greek, and Latin into English so that once again Christian people might hear the Scriptures in their own tongue. I have written these sermons for those who "push the plough" and for those who wish to hear the message in their own tongue. If my sermons help laity to be shaped by the Word, I shall be most grateful.

The following sermons move from the anticipation of Advent to the manifestation of Epiphany. They are intended to help the church understand itself and its mission through the message of these significant seasons.

This project would not have been possible without the infinite patience of my daughters, Melanie and Heather; my wife, Janene; and the able assistance of my perceptive, gifted and compassionate secretary, Mary Ann Haney. Their help, along with the tolerance of Belmont United Methodist Church, has enabled this modest book to come into being.

Shaped by the Future

For our children, Christmas is in the distant future; for adults, Christmas is just over the fence. For youngsters Christmas is a long journey; for grown-ups, it is just around the corner.

When I was a child, I thought December was the longest month of the entire year. I would get a commercial calendar and "X" off the days, hoping that such "X's" would somehow hasten the coming of Christmas. The closer I got to Christmas, the farther away it seemed. Christmas Eve felt like the longest day of the entire year.

When we become adults, Christmas comes too fast. Time rushes by. There is so much to do in so few days. There are gifts to buy, ceremonies to arrange, families to entertain, courtesies to care for, and protocol to move through. Christmas seems all too immediate and all too soon.

For children and adults, the coming of December twenty-fifth shapes our lives between the First Sunday in Advent and Christmas Day. It determines how we will live between "now" and "then".

In 1966, I was the pastor of St. Luke's United Methodist Church in Memphis, Tennessee. On a spring Thursday afternoon the White House called to tell us that the Vice President of the United States would be worshiping at St. Luke's Church the following Sunday morning. From Thursday afternoon until 10:50 a.m. Sunday morning, Mr. Humphrey's expected visit gave shape to our actions as a congregation. His coming determined how we would spend those few brief days. We knew that we must be ready for his arrival.

The earliest Christians earnestly believed that their lives were shaped by the Second Coming of Christ. They were convinced of their need to be ready for Christ's arrival, just as St. Luke's Church knew that it must be ready for the Vice President's visit. This conviction was one of the towering marks of the early church.

If we believe that the Son of man is coming, then that belief will determine how we live in the present. But if we do not believe that the Son of man is coming, we will shape the present like the past. Or, we will shape the present as if nothing is about to happen.

Matthew did not want his church to forget that the Son of man would come again! He used powerful imagery to nail that expectation to the minds of his readers. Matthew said that we should be alert to the arrival of Christ. In fact, he said we should spend our time watching and waiting for the advent of Christ. No one knows when He will come — not the angels, not even those who appear to be closest to God. Not one person will know the day nor the hour. Therefore, Jesus said that His followers should be forever ready because the Son of man would be coming at an hour that was least expected.

Matthew's teaching cannot be ignored. But many contemporary Christians are either too liberal or too modern to believe in Christ's Second Coming. Not many of us believe he will pop out of the sky onto a shopping mall parking lot. Nor do many of us hold the notion of him zipping through the clouds and landing in the center of Disney World — or worse, in the auditorium of the Thomas Road Baptist Church.

After all, we live for more proximate goals. Our lives are governed by goals and objectives which will help us to shape the future. We have graduate schools of business to teach us how to invent the future. Modern people believe that we can shape the future. But the First Sunday of Advent teaches us another lesson. It teaches what Matthew taught: we, as

Christians, are shaped by the future which comes to us.

I have a friend whose son is a student in a faraway college. This young freshman had not been home since he left in mid-August, but he was expected to return for Thanksgiving. Prior to his homecoming, the family spent their energy getting ready for his arrival. For days, the family anticipated the coming of their child. Preparations were made. His favorite foods were prepared. His room was spruced up and made ready. Members of the family planned to be home for his visit. The actions of the family had meaning and purpose because their present had been shaped by a future event. Likewise, if we believe in the coming of the Kingdom of God, then the church will try to live every day in anticipation of that event.

But as we all know, to prepare for a future event is difficult if we do not know when the event will occur. If we did not know when Christmas would come, then it would be difficult to shape our lives around that expectation. If we did not know when our daughter would be returning home from a long journey, then it would be hard to prepare for her homecoming.

This was precisely the problem of the early church. First-century Christians believed that the Christ who had come before would come again, but they did not know when. They lived in tension between the past Incarnation of Christ and the future consummation of all things in Christ at the end of time. How to live in the "meantime" remained a persistent issue of the early church.

And how to live in the meantime is our problem today! How are we to live if we do not know when God in his power will come into the world? If we knew the Kingdom would be coming on a certain date, we could be more earnestly shaping our lives in light of that expectation. But since we do not know, how should we live? What should we do?

Some wait for the Second Coming of Christ by trying to guess the precise date of his advent. Anticipating the end of the world in 1975, twenty-four men, women, and children from Grannis, Arkansas, moved into one tiny house and waited there for ten months. The end did not come as they had expected, and they were evicted for not paying their rent.

In 1986 a man named Richard Kieninger of Garland, Texas, organized a group of people to survive the calamities of the end of time. On May 5, 2000, Kieninger's followers plan to witness the last day from a dirt pile.

Similarly in 1525, a German preacher named Stoeffler predicted the end of the world by flood. All of his parishioners built boats and rafts to survive the end. When the flood did not come, they threw Herr Stoeffler into a deep pond.

Such was the case on October 22, 1844. The followers of William Miller, a farmer turned preacher, donned white ascension robes and waited on a hilltop for the Second Coming of Christ. When Christ did not come, they adjusted their beliefs and formed what is now known as the Seventh Day Adventist Church.

Jesus said that we should not wait by trying to guess the date. Said Jesus, "No one knows, not even the angels of heaven." He wanted his followers to be ready for the day of the coming of the Lord. He said that we must be ready because the Son of man is coming at an hour we least expect.

Jesus' call is clear. He calls his followers to expect the end to come at any moment. Our Lord challenges us to watch as we would if we knew the end was just around the corner.

Imagine two houses in a neighborhood. One is ready, and one is not. One house believes that the end will never come. The other house believes that the end could be today or tomorrow. The first house believes that tomorrow will be just like today; this household lives for itself. The second house believes the future belongs to the Lord; this household lives to make the future God intended. One house watches, and the other does not.

Without a doubt, we should live by watching and being ready. Watching, according to Matthew and Mark, does not mean observing in a detached way. Watching, in this context, means to do something. It means to be engaged in the world.

It means to be involved in the pain and the hope of others. It is the difference between watching a "so-so" television program and sitting by the bedside of a child who has a life-threatening illness. While watching a television program, one can remain neutral or impassive. While watching a sick child, one becomes involved in that child's pain. The congregation that I serve operates a shelter for homeless people every Friday night. Members of our Homeless Committee take turns spending the night in the shelter. Recently one of these volunteers told me, "Pastor, it's not difficult to stay awake, but it is hard to watch with engagement." He was saying that it is *not* easy to be involved in the pain of homeless people. It is one thing to watch from a distance, but it is another to be involved.

As Christians, we have the opportunity to "watch with engagement" daily. For most of us, this means serving God through loving others as we go about our daily tasks. Watching for the Son of man does not mean putting on a big display. According to Matthew, the Kingdom will come in all of its power and glory to the two men working in the field and to the two women grinding at the mill.

And, that is the good news. While going about our tasks, we do not have to do anything spectacular. We should simply live today expecting the end to be just around the corner. If we believe that God's tomorrow will be the end of war, of racial distinctions, of hunger, of hate, of greed, and of barriers — all of which keep God's children from being equal — then we, as followers of Christ, will live in light of that tomorrow. The future will shape us.

Repentance

One of the towering marks of this age is the absence of guilt. Not many people would deny that startling fact. Some are pleased that guilt has been dethroned; others see it as a bad sign.

The absence of guilt is one of the reasons that it is difficult to talk about repentance. If there is no feeling of guilt, the need for repentance is greatly minimized, if not extinct.

A few years ago, I was involved in experimental worship. I tried many innovative ways to enable worship to be more experiential and less stilted. At one such service, I invited those in attendance to write down something they would like to repent. The worshipers were then instructed to seal the slip of paper in a small envelope provided by the church, and to address it back to themselves. The envelopes would be returned to each person just before the New Year. After the service, a man approached me with some distaste for my request. He labeled the exercise "slick" and "manipulative". "And besides that," he said, "I do not need to repent of anything. What does repentance mean anyway?"

For many, repentance is *a word that belongs to yesterday.* It is equated with sackcloth and ashes, mourner's benches, and nearby church confessionals. At best, repentance is a slippery word. Hearing it or saying it does not form any meaning in the consciousness of people. If a word has lost its meaning, then it does not carry any freight. If it is not understood, then there is nothing to unpack.

15

For some, repentance is *something that is done when one gets caught*. It is something one does if one is caught having an affair, cheating on the Internal Revenue Service, having one's hand in the till, or illegally recruiting college athletes. When caught, an individual will often repent by saying a heartfelt "I'm sorry." But repentance is far more than blurting out "I'm sorry" when one gets caught at something deemed wrong by conventional society.

For others, repentance is *something that a person does when he or she is in a bind*. For example, a job loss, a death in a family, or a major disappointment may cause an individual to feel that he or she is in an eternal pinch. Repentance then becomes a way of extricating oneself from a jam which may or may not be of one's making.

Nor is repentance merely *turning over a new leaf*. Sunday afternoon and evening represent my favorite time of the week. With the pressure of Sunday morning lifted, the afternoon and evening move at a more leisurely pace. A fire is built. The large Sunday paper is carefully read. My Sunday suit is exchanged for old "dog clothes." I enjoy this time of the week because it is like starting all over again. It is like putting a clean page in the typewriter. It is like the feeling one has on December thirty-first every year. But, repentance is more than starting afresh.

I took Matthew's account of John the Baptizer to an adult Sunday school class in our congregation. After giving some background information and interpretation, I asked the class to help me prepare a sermon on the theme of repentance. I asked, "If you were in my place, what would you say to this congregation about repentance?" Blank, sheepish stares lined the faces of the class members. One person responded, "We are like the people in John's day. We are so close to it that we cannot hear the message."

"It is like preaching to the choir," another said. "No one listens because we have been conditioned to hear something else."

Yet another said, "Repentance is something we do in corporate prayer, not something we do in our hearts."

Repentance is more than mumbling the prayer of General Confession on Sunday morning. Repentance goes far deeper than going through some prescribed behavior when one gets caught, is in a bind, or wants to start with a clean slate. In fact, John the Baptizer gave a strange twist to repentance. In most of Scripture, repentance expresses a variety of ideas: (a) a change of mind, (b) the feeling of regret or remorse, or (c) in the ethico-religious sense, the act of turning away from and back to God. The last of these is the most prominent and most significant in the Bible. In both the Hebrew Bible and the New Testament, repentance refers to humankind's need to "turn away from" and to "turn back" to God. However, the emphasis may rest on the negative side. One must pay for having turned away from God. John the Baptizer, the waymaker of the Messiah, hit a different note. He said, "Repent, for the Kingdom of Heaven is at hand." Dressed in strange garb and eating a trail mix of locusts and wild honey, he came preaching sermons about how to prepare for the coming One. He preached that people should prepare for the coming One by repenting and by bearing fruit worthy of repentance.

In this context, repentance does not mean to change one's mind. Nor does it mean to feel sorry for one's sins. Nor does it mean to make bold resolves never to commit the same transgressions. Instead, in Matthew's Gospel, repentance means to turn toward the One who is yet to come. John the Baptizer wanted his audience to turn their lives toward the Messiah who was just around the corner.

This kind of repentance is not negative, dour, and longfaced. It is not the kind of repentance that causes one to put on sackcloth and ashes. Rather, this understanding of repentance turns one toward a new reality which is about to break into the present reality where death and oppression reign. John the Baptizer invites people who are on the edge of this new reality to get ready and to be prepared for the new age. He

does not ride the same old horse with the same old words —
"Repent, you bums!" He does not hit his listeners over the
head with a saddlebag full of sin and guilt. Instead, John the
Baptizer invites men and women to get ready for the new age
which will be inaugurated with the coming of Christ. Matthew
wants us to understand that to repent means to turn ourselves
in the direction of the Christ.

In 1972, my wife and I had the opportunity to worship in
Shepherd's Field, which is located just outside the city of Bethlehem. It was a few weeks before Christmas and we were
gathered with Christians from all over the world. It was one
of those brisk nights when the cold was pushed by a gusty north
wind. The blackened sky was dotted with a multitude of spar-
kling stars. Rocks cracked and moved under our feet. Off in
the distance, we could see the lit skyline of Bethlehem where
Mary had gone to give birth.

While standing in Shepherd's Field, we sang the songs of
Christmas, participated in the liturgy, and heard the proclamation of the Word. It was one of those rare moments when
life was filled with awe and mystery. As I worshiped, I did
not look up to God and say, "God, look at how virtuous I
am." Nor did I utter, "God, pat me on the back for all the
good things that I have done." I did not pretend by saying,
"God, look at all of my accomplishments. Aren't you proud
of me?" Instead, I found myself turning toward Christ. The
more I turned toward him, the more I found myself repenting
my sins. That is the way it works. The more we turn away from
Christ, the more we become enslaved to the power of sin; the
more we turn toward Christ, the more we become free from
the power and bondage of sin. To be certain, it is turning
toward Christ that enables us to repent.

To understand repentance as orienting our lives toward
Christ is to understand that repentance is not something done
only during the "Shepherd's Field" experiences of life. Repenting in this fashion is a daily affair. Turning toward Christ daily
helps us to revise our past. This season, like no other, provides

for us the opportunity to turn our lives toward the One who came and is yet to come. This "hope" is worth pondering. Every morning, a congregation in my neighborhood holds an Order for Morning Prayer. The pastor of the church often speaks about how important it is to give people the opportunity to practice repentance and confession every day. We need to turn our lives toward Christ daily by using the Prayer Book, kneeling at a prie-dieu, making the Sign of the Cross, and dipping our fingers in a bowl of water. Daily repentance has the strength to break the power of sin.

But what are the signs of repentance? How do we know that it is real? According to Matthew, it is not lineage or credentials. Instead, it is fruit-bearing that is the sign of true repentance. The evidence of repentance is to be found in the fruit that is brought forth in our lives. Repentance is a positive act — something which does some good.

A woman comes to the prayer chapel of our church every day. About the same time every morning, she can be seen kneeling with her hands folded and her head bowed. After turning toward Christ in prayer, she goes to a nearby food distribution center where she loads her car with trays of food to deliver to people in need. Her daily routine is no big deal to her. She never calls attention to it. Her life bears fruit as naturally as a new shoot emerges from the root of a freshly hewn tree. Repentance, as turning toward the One who is yet to come, does not lead to self-centeredness. We are free to serve and to love.

The following letter from an unknown source tells a similar story:

Dear _____,
   I appreciated very much your gentle letter about the Central Shelter. For me, it was the location for an occasion of grace which I wish to share with you.
   In December 1981 I became a Catholic. Prior to that, I had been a theistic liberal. But my progress to this point is too long to tell. In my general confession, which I had to

make prior to my entrance into the church, I left out one serious sin involving a relationship I was in at the time. Although I had tried very hard to justify this relationship, I wasn't ready to let it go yet. But a month or so later, it still hung heavy on my conscience, and I knew that I had to give it up and make full peace with God. I started going to daily Mass at Immaculate Conception. After Communion every day for a week, I prayed that I would meet an unfamiliar priest to whom I could make a full confession. I didn't want to expose myself in this way to my parish, although I told him later.

Do you remember that monster snowstorm we had that January? I was one of those stuck that night in downtown Atlanta after the buses had stopped running. I didn't know where to go at first, but I finally thought of the shelter at Central which I had read about in the Georgia Bulletin. I had always intended to volunteer there, but I had never called. So I went there seeking shelter, but I was accepted immediately as a volunteer. Because of the bad weather, only two volunteers had been able to make it that night — and one of them was a priest from Sacred Heart. I asked him to hear my confession that night, and he did. But since it had been a busy night, it was 2:00 a.m. before he had time for me.

The next morning, I waited only five minutes for my bus to come. I was the only passenger. After I got home, I started to make breakfast, and as I cooked, I talked to God. I thanked him for his peace and for getting me home safely. I had gone over to the pantry to get something, when, all at once, I was overcome by a deep awareness of God's love for me. His love was like a taste of the joy of heaven, and I knew throughout every part of me what love really was. I haven't begun to describe this experience to you. I don't know how. But I realized then that I had to move toward God's love any way that I could. No human love would ever be sufficient. From that day forward, I began to pray for a vocation to religious life, even though at the time this seemed impossible because of my background.

To make a long story short, on February 12, 1984, I am

entering the Carmelite Monastery at Danvers, Massachusetts. They are a cloistered, contemplative community whose apostolate is prayer.

I know that you are not Catholic, but I felt that you would like to hear of yet another example of the Lord's gracious, merciful presence among us.

Please know that the Central Presbyterian Shelter has its own prayer-friend from now on. You all will be constantly remembered by myself and by my community. I hope you will pray for us.

In Christ's love,

This letter makes one want to get the decorations out. Like its unidentified writer, when we try to move toward the love of Christ, things begin to happen. Life takes new directions. Life takes on new joy and vitality.

A key layperson in my church recently said, "If we are not careful, John the Baptizer will take all of the fun out of Christmas." I think my friend is dead wrong. Heeding the preaching of John the Baptizer will restore joy to Christmas. What better way to prepare than to turn one's life toward Christ and to bear fruit as a sign of repentance? That is the way to prepare for a real Christmas. And that is what most of us want because we are bone tired of Christmas the way it is. John the Baptizer's preaching calls us not to the way Christmas is, but to the way it is meant to be.

Responding to
What We Hear and See

In the semantics of the church, doubt has been a negative word. It is rarely used in a favorable way. Faith, not doubt, is the great word of the church.

As I stand here every Sunday morning and look into your up-lifted faces, you look so proper, so content, so believing. You seem to be so certain, so full of faith, and so free of doubt.

But, I have a suspicion that the way you look is not the way you are. Beneath the skins of many of you there is planted the seed of honest doubt. Perhaps you do not share these feelings with anyone; but your doubts are there, and they are real. Your worship does not express your doubts, uncertainties, and skepticism. In facing this situation, all of us at times cry out with the man in the Gospel, "Lord, I believe; help thou my unbelief." This capacity to doubt can often lead to some of life's most profound questions.

Such was the case with John the Baptizer. His question — "Are you he who is to come, or shall we look for another?" — grew not out of his uncertainty, but out of his doubt. John the Baptizer had heard about the words and deeds of Jesus, but what he had heard did not square with his expectation of the Messiah.

After all, Jesus was born not to royalty, but to a peasant woman. He functioned not as a military ruler, but as a servant.

He came not as a judge, but as a forgiving redeemer. He did not bring heavenly condemnation; he brought divine love. He did not associate with the religious establishment, but he went from village to village associating with the rubbish heap of humanity. He spent his time and energy with the least and the lost. He was most concerned with the powerless: the blind and the lame, the lepers and the deaf, and the poor and the outcast. And Jesus dared to teach that the weak occupied the most important place in the Kingdom of God.

John the Baptizer became confused about the way in which Jesus acted out his messiahship. He had doubts about the validity of his contemporary, Jesus of Nazareth. His skepticism caused him to send one of his buddies to Jesus with the question: "Are you he who is to come, or shall we look for another?" Like others in the New Testament, John the Baptizer was not positive. Oh, to be sure, there were fleeting moments of recognition. Mary thought Jesus was a gardener. Those on the road to Emmaus never did recognize him. Even his closest disciples were not certain if he was or was not the true Messiah.

That John the Baptizer had doubts about the messiahship of Jesus is revealed in his question: "Are you the one who is to come, or shall we look for another?" His question is not clear, either in what is being asked or why. But like all good questions, it shoves the reader into deeper regions of thought.

On the other hand, Jesus gave a straightforward answer to the question raised by the disciples of John the Baptizer. Without equivocation he said, "Go and tell John what you hear and see: the blind receive their sight and the lame walk, lepers are cleansed and the deaf hear, and the dead are raised up and the poor have good news preached to them. And blessed is he who takes no offense at me."

The answer that Jesus gave was plain and simple. In essence he said, "You go and tell John that he will have to respond to me based on what he sees and hears." Jesus was asking John the Baptizer to look at His deeds and to listen to His words as a way of getting an answer to his question: "Are you the one who is to come, or shall we look for another?"

And that is one of the ways we will have to respond to the One who comes to us during this season. We will be forced to respond based on what we *see* and *hear*. The coming One will not force himself on us. No other person has the power to make us decide. Our response will finally rest upon what we hear with our ears and see with our eyes. That is the way it was for John the Baptizer, and that is the way it must be for you and me.

But, there is a grave danger. The danger is that we will look in the wrong places, and we will listen to the wrong voices. The danger is that we will look to places of power, privilege, and prestige for a sign of Jesus' coming. But, the chances are that we will not see him in rooms filled with people who wear Gucci shoes; Hart, Shaffner & Marx suits; and Gant shirts.

Instead, Jesus will be found where sight is given to the blind, legs to the lame, hearing to the deaf, and new life to the dead. The Messiah will be found whenever and wherever the powerless are given power. If we want to respond to the signs of Christ's presence in today's world, we will look at those places where the weak are being made strong.

Examples abound. We do not have to take a sacred trip to a special place in order to see the powerless getting power. It is happening all over town and right here in this church.

One Tuesday evening in 1987 was one of the greatest nights of the year for our congregation. It was the annual International Christmas dinner party. Tables and chairs for one hundred and twenty people had been set up, and still more had to be added. Almost every square inch of the tables had been covered with food representing forty-two countries.

When our guests arrived, some were decked out in their native dress; others wore Americanized clothing. Many spoke in their native tongue. However, since many of those who attended registered in the congregation's English as a Second

Language Program, some guests spoke either broken or fluent English. The world community miraculously squeezed into the Fellowship Hall. It was a joyful event, as joyful as any that I had hoped to experience during Advent.

As I stood in the winding food line, I had a conversation with a woman from Brazil. She said, "Pastor, I want to thank your church for having English as a Second Language and for having this dinner. It is hard for us to be away from home. Our loved ones are so far away. Often, we are so lonely that we cry at night. But, when we come to Elizabeth Duncan's English class and when we come here for these dinners, we feel warm and strong." In her face and in her words, I saw the face and heard the words of the One who is to come. Because of people like Dot, Elizabeth, and Gordon, this woman has been given the power to do what she has to do. In the life of that weak woman who has been made strong, one can see a sign of the coming One.

It happens all the time. Weakness becomes strength for the prisoner who receives a visit, for the homeless family who is given a night's lodging, for the student whose teacher stays after school to tutor without compensation, for the sick person who receives a brief but sincere visit from a good friend, for the hungry child who receives nourishment because of U.N.I.C.E.F., and for all of us when summits bring us one step nearer to peace without arms. Even as Christ is present every time the bread is broken and the wine is served, so is Christ present every time the powerless are given power to stand up and face life with some love and dignity.

The first danger, then, is that we will not respond to the coming One because we look to the places of power and privilege and not to those life situations where the weak are made stronger.

The second danger is that we will not respond to the coming One because we do not hear his Voice. And the reason that we do not hear his Voice is that we will spend this season listening to the wrong voices. Instead of responding to his Voice, we will respond to the voices of a crass, commercial Christmas. We will respond to the voices of buzzing cash registers, bustling crowds, the discordant secular hype. During this time of the year, there are so many voices that appear to be so promising, so alluring, and so full of power. The danger is that we will listen only to those voices that promise us more privilege, security, and power. The danger is that we will listen only to those voices that teach us to adhere to the "Doctrine of More." And, the greater danger is that we will not hear the Voice of the coming One beyond and above the noisy crowd.

If we get caught up in the busy trivia of this season, then we will rush headlong into oblivion. Only when we are alone, quiet and listening to the other Voice, does the inner rhythm begin to flow. Only then do the senses come closer to realization. Only then does one begin to hear the Voice beyond the screaming voices of mass culture.

But, there is an even greater danger than the risk of looking in the wrong places and listening to the wrong voices. It is the danger of not looking afresh at what Jesus did and not listening anew to what he said. One of the ways that we can prepare for Christmas is to study again the deeds of Jesus and to read again the words of Jesus. Like John the Baptizer, we need to respond based on what we see and hear in the life of Jesus of Nazareth. If we do not study Jesus' deeds and listen to his words, then we will make the coming One into something that he is not. The following poem is an example of how far afield we can go:

Jesus, what have you done to us?
We wanted a pet kitten
And you turned into a tiger.
We liked you the way you were.
Why couldn't you leave us alone?

We wanted you to show up when we
wanted you to make us feel good.

We wanted a pretty church for weddings
and baptisms and funerals.
We wanted the cute Easter bunny hopping
around the lawn.
We thought religion was good for the
kiddies.

Now all of a sudden you've turned against us.
We wanted peace and you brought us a sword.
Things were going along all right.
Then you got interested in the poor people.
Now they're strutting around like they
Are going to inherit the earth.

Now all of a sudden you tell us
To love our enemies.
Do you know what will happen if we do?
They will nail our hide to the wall
And what will we do then, keep on praying for them?

We liked you when you were a little boy
Gentle, meek and mild, cooing in your cradle.
All those nice shepherds and angels,
And we felt just awful about King Herod.

Look at all we did for you.
We made a national holiday in your honor.
We built big industries around it — Christmas cards,
Toy machine guns for the kiddies
And all those fancy gift-wrapped whiskey bottles.

We built pretty churches in your honor,
Stained glass, organs, the works,
And when the people moved away from the riff raff,
The church followed them
Straight out into the suburbs.

Looking at all we've done for you, Jesus,
Why can't you leave us alone?

We've got enough troubles now.
Why do you keep pricking our conscience?
What do you want for Christmas, our hearts?

Because of his doubts, John the Baptizer introduced us to the One who is to come. And like him, we will have to respond on the basis of what we hear and see.

As we move swiftly through the rituals of the season, let us not fail to look and to listen. Not looking and not listening might cause us to miss the point of it all, and that would be a sad and terrible thing.

Love Transcending Law and Custom

Joseph was in a bind! Mary, his betrothed, had become pregnant. Both law and custom were on his side. Joseph could have broken his vow to become her husband, thereby putting Mary to shame. Or, he could have divorced her quietly, thereby putting her in an untenable position. He could have charged her with infidelity, thus repudiating her and reducing her to a life of shame.

While Joseph was trying to decide what to do, an angel of the Lord appeared to him in a dream and said: "Joseph, Son of David, do not fear to take Mary your wife, for that which is conceived in her is of the Holy Spirit; she will bear a son, and you shall call his name Jesus, for he will save his people from their sins."

According to the customs and standards of his day, Joseph had every right to divorce Mary quietly. Law and tradition were his allies. All of Joseph's customers would have understood. Not one person in the village of Nazareth would have argued with him. He could have slipped out of a most difficult situation.

But instead of taking the easy way out of his bind, Joseph heeded what the angel of the Lord commanded and took Mary as his wife. Instead of trying to find some way to separate himself from Mary, Joseph loved her and cared for her. For

Joseph, care was more important than conventional expectations. Compassion was more important than honored rights. Love, justice, and a sense of responsibility were more important than tradition and law.

Every now and then we see a modern-day Joseph — a person for whom love takes precedent over rules and conventional morality. Every now and then we see a person whose vision of life has been lifted above "what everybody else does." Every now and then we see a person for whom compassion is more important than legality.

The December 7, 1987, issue of *The New York Times* carried a story about a contemporary Joseph. The story took place in Enniskillen, North Ireland, where the killing of one Irish person by another is a routine part of life. So commonplace is killing there that it is unusual when the loss of innocent life causes people to stop and actually wonder whether the long, coarse weave of vendettas and grievances might be altered.

People in Belfast, Dublin, and London started trying to answer that all-important question after eleven Irish civilians were killed in Enniskillen on November 8, 1987. Among those killed was twenty-year-old Marie Wilson, a student nurse mortally wounded when she was crushed by a wall in which the Irish Republican Army had hidden a powerful bomb. The I.R.A. later insisted that they intended for the bomb to kill security forces at a memorial service, not civilians.

Given the normal pace of Irish atrocities, the story of Ms. Wilson's demise might have slipped from general sight within a few brief days. But the citizens of Ireland talked about her tragic death for days, even weeks.

As Ms. Wilson lay dying under the rubble, she held the hand of her father, Gordon, who had also been buried beneath the pile of debris. "She had been screaming at times, then reassuring me," Gordon Wilson recalled, his right arm in a sling, his hand groping uselessly as he talked. "She said, 'Daddy, I love you very much,' " he continued in a tone remarkable in its gentleness. "Those were the last words she spoke."

Gordon Wilson stunned the British Isles when he said, "I bear no ill will at all." In the first angry hours after the bombing, Mr. Wilson's reaction was to pray for his daughter's killers.

His statement is even more extraordinary when put in context of other black-night tragedies which now have a roll-call familiarity: the "Bloody Sunday" shooting of thirteen Catholic nationalist civil rights marchers by British security forces in Londonderry in 1972; the bombing by a Protestant loyalist who killed fifteen Catholic nationalists in McGurk's Barroom in Belfast sixteen years ago; and for the pro-British loyalists, the Birmingham pub bombings by the I.R.A. that killed twenty-one people fourteen years ago. The bombing at Enniskillen will soon fade into just another line in this list of troubles.

However, Mr. Wilson was not interested in trying to fit his daughter into the long list of political atrocities. "Marie's last words were about life," he said, slowly lilting her name, "MAH-re," in Irish "It would be no way for me to remember her by having words of hatred in my mouth.

"But, I tell you this," he said, "A woman, someone I would call a sharp-edged Protestant, came to my door sobbing after Marie died. The woman said the tragedy had 'softened her heart'. Now that has to be good," said the father, pondering the value of Marie's life and death. "That has to be good."

In Gordon Wilson, we have a contemporary Joseph. His attitude goes far beyond the attitudes expressed by custom and tradition. Mirroring compassion was far more important to him than speaking for the collective voice of a society gone mad.

The biblical story of Joseph makes the heart grow soft. This is so because Joseph was true to his understanding of what God expected of him. He did as God commanded when law, tradition, and custom gave him permission to take a road much wider and much less difficult. Instead of taking the wide path, Joseph cooperated with the action of God in human history.

He did as the Angel requested He named his son Jesus, which is a Greek form of the Hebrew "Joshua" meaning "he shall save". As the ancient saviors of Israel saved their people from foreign oppressors, so Jesus was to save his people. Joseph, as the result of the divine oracle vouchsafed to him in his dream, terminated his betrothal by taking Mary home to live in his house.

There is a lot ot talk today about what makes Christmas. Newspaper and television advertisements coax people into believing that they can have a real Christmas by going to a festive shopping center, eating at trendy restaurants, or watching glittering "Christmas programs" on television. Others believe that Christmas is made by the fastidious keeping of time-honored family rituals, such as, sentimental ornaments on just the right tree, eating food from a menu which has been handed down from generation to generation, or by visiting the same relatives at precisely the same time on Christmas Day. Some believe that Christmas is made by purchasing a uniquely special gift for every relative, friend, and acquaintance. To be sure, all of these contribute to our cultural understanding of Christmas.

But the answer to "What makes a real Christmas?" must be found in human history. That is what Joseph did. And, in a very real sense, it was the theology of Joseph which made possible the first Christmas. If Joseph had not cooperated with God's action in human history, the birth of Jesus would have been quite different.

The witness of Joseph calls us to cooperate with God's work in today's world. It calls us to respond to God's action among us.

Joseph, not having all of the evidence and knowledge of the future, decided to do more than law and custom required. He elected to do more than was expected of him. He let justice and compassion guide his decision about his pregnant betrothed. He was pulled, not by the strength of custom, but by the law of love.

But, isn't it strange that during this season we are more prone to be like Joseph than during the rest of the year? During these last days of Advent, we are more apt to practice mercy than at any other time of the year. The questions that we raised from the first of last January until just before Thanksgiving do not seem to be very appropriate when Christmas is just around the corner.

All of the rest of the year we ask questions: "Do they really deserve it?", "Are they really hungry?", or "How do people get their lives so messed up?" Or we make comments like: "All we owe people is an opportunity", "Let's give to those who deserve it", "Let's help those who help themselves", or "How much longer are we going to try to turn our plowshares and pruning hooks into swords?"

But, it is true — people start acting strange around the Fourth Sunday of Advent. The most hard-nosed and opinionated start scurrying around to find people who need to be helped. The most tight-fisted search for places to give away some hard cash. The busiest people in town take time to ring bells on street corners. Agencies and churches get calls from people who actually want to lend a hand. Volunteers seem to pour out of the woodwork. In large measure, those who fill the pews of the church today are those who do not darken the church door during the rest of the year. The Incarnation seems to call us to rise above the way we live the rest of the year. The strangest people seem to live an understanding of love which transcends law and custom.

The way we cooperate with God's intentions during this season tells us that we are capable of responding. It tells us that by God's grace we can live by a standard of love which transcends tradition and custom. This is the season that we can join God in what God is trying to do. It is because of Emmanuel — "God is with us."

Away with the Stable

If we could change some of our images of the Christmas story, it would mean more to us. If we could get the birth narrative straight, it would not be diminished but enriched.

Luke records the incident of Christ's birth in a very simple and a very beautiful way: "[Mary] gave birth to her first-born son and wrapped him in swaddling cloths, and laid him in a manger, because there was no place for them in the inn." Regardless of the stories that we have been told and hear about the little Bethlehem hotel being full, in spite of all of the criticism that we have heaped upon the innkeeper because he sent pregnant Mary outside to a cold stable, and no matter how many stables are erected in homes and on church parking lots — there is the possibility that Jesus was not born in a stable. The Gospel of Luke does not mention Mary and Joseph arriving at Bethlehem at the last minute. Nor does Luke say that they scurried around to find a place to lodge because the baby was about to be born. Luke simply says "while they were there," as though they had arrived several days ahead of Jesus' birth.

Luke makes no mention of a stable. He merely comments on the fact that Mary "gave birth to her first-born son and wrapped him in swaddling cloths and laid him in a manger." Luke wrote not one word about a hotel or an innkeeper who cold-heartedly turned the family away. There is no way to know how many Christmas pageants have portrayed the bad

37

innkeeper who turned Mary and Joseph away from the door. According to Luke's Gospel, that hard innkeeper and his tiny inn did not exist.

Luke tells the story another way.

In Luke's Gospel the word which is typically translated as "inn" is the Greek word *kataluma*. It is interesting to note that in the story of the Good Samaritan, Luke does not use the word *kataluma* to describe the inn to which the beaten man was taken. He uses another word to describe the place of lodging beside the Jericho Road. However, Luke tells about Jesus sending two of his disciples to find a *kataluma* for the serving of the Last Supper. Thus in Luke, the word *kataluma* literally means a "guest room." As Luke tells the story of the nativity, it is just possible that a proper translation would be something like this: "She gave birth to her first-born son and laid him in a manger because there was no place for them in the guest room."

Logic suggests that there is some basis for this translation. Bethlehem probably had no inn or hotel since it was only six miles from Jerusalem, a mere two-hour walk. Furthermore, Bethlehem was not located on a main highway. The Roman roads in that region bypassed the City of David and went directly to Jerusalem. In all probability, this small village had no need for an inn.

If Mary and Joseph had come here for a census, it is not unlikely that they had relatives living in Bethlehem with whom they could have stayed. It is possible that the carpenter from Nazareth and his young wife arrived a few days before the birth of their son and found the *kataluma*, the "guest room", already occupied by other relatives and guests. Since there was no room in the guest room, they might have lodged in the main room with the homeowner and his family. Thus, it may be that Jesus was not born in the inn or guest room, but right out in the middle of the main room of the house.

We cannot fully appreciate the message of Luke unless we

first understand the configuration of a Palestinian house. In those days a peasant's house was a simple, one-room affair. A man, his wife, their family, and all of their belongings were concentrated in one main room. If the owner of the house had sufficient resources, he would build a small room, or *kataluma*. It was not uncommon for travelers to be offered a couple's guest room or inn as a place of lodging.

In the dead cold of winter, it was not uncommon for a Palestinian family to bring into their house all of the livestock. This provided shelter for the animals, and the heat of the beasts' bodies provided warmth for all who resided in the house. Usually the central room had an upper and a lower level. The family lived on the upper level while the cattle were kept on the lower level, possibly a foot or two lower than the rest of the house. On the step, next to where the cattle were lodged, there would have been a manger area. The location for the manger was a place scooped out to create a trough where the cattle could be fed. It was in that manger area, right in the middle of the house, that Palestinian women gave birth to their children so that the newborn might have the comfort of the manger's straw.

Listen carefully to what Luke is saying to his reader when the story is told in this way. He said that Mary gave birth to Jesus right in the middle of the house because there was no room in the *kataluma*, or "guest room." Luke wanted his readers to hear something very special. He wanted his words to convey the notion that Jesus, the Son of God, was born, not off in the guest room, but right in the midst of smelly hay, snorting animals, anxious on-lookers, and the tenderness and love of the family circle. Jesus, our Savior, was born just like all other children of that day. He was tenderly placed precisely where all other children of that day were cradled. When the Magi arrived from afar, they came, as Matthew said, "into the house [where] they saw the child with Mary, his mother." (Matthew 2:11)

If we experience the birth of Christ on Christmas Eve, it will not be in the guest rooms of our lives, but right in the middle of it all. We will experience his birth right in the midst of people who love each other. We will feel his birth not in the *kataluma*, but in the pain of the world where his influence still says, "be reconciled to God." (2 Corinthians 5:20) We will see his yearning to be born again in the Middle East where his voice still cries out for peace and good will on earth. We will find him, not in the side rooms of life, but with the poor, the imprisoned, and the hungry. If we listen closely, we can still hear his voice saying, "As you did it to one of the least of these my brethren, you did this to me." (Matthew 25:40)

One of the traditions in my family is to gather at my wife's home on Christmas Day to break bread and open gifts. For almost twenty-three years I have joined my family in that ritual. Until my wife's grandfather died, one of the tender moments of every December twenty-fifth had been Granddaddy's prayer before the Christmas feast. All of the family would gather in one room, and Granddaddy, his voice quiet but confident, would pray the same prayer every year. "Help us," he would say, "not to forget the birth of the One whom we remember on this day." He would pray that simple prayer right in the midst of it all: the aroma of the almost-done turkey, the eager grandchildren, the large room littered with wrapping paper, and the growling stomachs and tender taste buds. Granddaddy had never heard of the *kataluma*, but he prayed as though Christ had not been pushed into the guest room of his life.

Frederick Buechner, a well-known writer and preacher, was invited to teach a course in preaching at a Protestant seminary. Uncertainty gripped him because he had never ventured into teaching homiletics. He began by teaching his students how to draft introductions, conclusions, and thesis statements. But toward the middle of the semester, he came to the silent conclusion that what he was teaching the students did not amount to very much. After apparent failure, he took a different approach. Instead of teaching the theory of preaching, he decided to teach his students about feelings. He said, "I tell them to pay special attention to those times when they find tears in their eyes.''

That's where Christ is born. If we want Christ to be born in the cradles of our hearts, we might do well to look for him in those experiences which cause emotions to surface in our eyes and in our hearts. If we want a new awareness of Christ's birth, we might give attention to those times when our heart skips, a knot lumps in our throat, and feeling pulses through our veins. Here, right in the middle of it all, is where Christ is born.

Why not do away with the stable? Doing away with the stable might shatter some of our fantasies and fairy tales, but it would make a difference in how we view the Incarnation. If Jesus was born like all other peasant children, the event of his birth becomes something very positive and powerful. It means that Jesus is one of us. It means that God is present in the events and lives of ordinary people.

When we possess the understanding that God surfaces in the commonplace, then we are never the same again. When we understand that God goes to any lengths to meet us in the "stuff" of life, then we know that we can never hide from God. To see God as absent from the "stuff" of life is to deny the Incarnation.

On Christmas Eve, more than any other night of the year, we know that the God of the Christian faith is not on the boundary of life. He is Emmanuel — "God with us." If we open our ears tonight, we can hear the God who has no voice and yet who speaks in everything that is — and who, most of all, speaks in the depths of our own being. We are the words of God.

The Message of Christmas

Christ was not born in the clean, sterile rooms of a local hospital. He was not born in the southeastern part of the United States. He was not Caucasian. He was not American.

His humble family was not known outside the city of Nazareth. We know very little about Joseph except that he was a carpenter, a just and honorable man of the house and lineage of David. We know very little of his mother, Mary. We do know that she probably belonged to the *anawiem*, the poor ones of Palestine, and we know that she was a very unlikely person to be the mother of Christ.

Hebrew was Christ's language for the acquisition of knowledge. Aramaic was his mode of everyday speech. English was unknown to him. Never did he travel more than a few miles from his home town. He knew absolutely nothing about modern medicine, science, or economics.

He never went to a barbershop. He did not wear tailor-made clothing. He had no public holdings, save a tunic and some sandals. We know that his associates were simple people: fishermen, merchants, tax-collectors, and prostitutes.

More than anyone else, the religious establishment stood against him. He was accused of "stirring up" the people or, as we would say, of being a rabble-rouser. He was often misunderstood. He was not followed by many, and he had very few people who supported him when the chips were down. Very few people stayed with him as he moved toward Golgotha. We know he was given a criminal's death, and he was mockingly called "the King of the Jews."

It is the birthday of this kind of man that we are now celebrating. According to our standards of success, mine and yours, Jesus was a flop at thirty-three. He didn't have many friends; he had no holdings; he had nothing in the bank; he had no rank or standing. According to the way we judge success, Jesus never made it. By our standards, he would clearly be classified as a failure. Simeon said that the Messiah's mission would be fulfilled, but it would only be fulfilled with suffering, opposition, rebuke and scorn.

Only a small portion of what Jesus said was ever retained on the printed page. Jesus himself never wrote a book. He never wrote a poem. He never wrote a song. As far as we know, he never wrote anything that was printed and handed down from one generation to the next. Out of all that he said and did — out of all the travels, all the stories, all the parables — only a very few are contained in the few short words of four brief gospels.

In spite of all these limitations, people from every part of the world are honoring him by celebrating his birth. His influence is more far-reaching and profound than all the parliaments that ever sat or all the navies that ever plied the oceans of the world. More paintings, more books, and more music have been created in honor of this man than in honor of any person who ever lived. In his name, the hungry are still fed, the naked are still clothed, the sick are still treated, the lonely are still visited, and the bound continue to be set free.

If I listen very closely today, I can hear the voices of millions stretching from Nashville to Hong Kong, and from Hong Kong to London, as they sing the immortal hymns of Christmas. If I feel deeply enough today, I can feel in my own life what Handel must have felt when he penned the *Messiah*. And if I need more proof, I can listen to saints, martyrs, and average people as they relate how the inward presence of this one man has changed their lives.

Christmas, more than any other time of the year, makes us want to put into practice the principle by which Jesus lived and for which he died. It is a principle which is universal and proven true. Anyone can live by it. Anyone regardless of his or her skin pigmentation, speech, or national origin can live by this principle of love, if he or she so chooses. This principle of love, as lived out in the life of Jesus, can be as easily understood by a PhD from Vanderbilt as a poor and illiterate person from the slums of North Nashville. This principle of love, as articulated and lived out by Jesus, is so powerful that it can reunite a broken family, reunite a neighborhood, and bring distant parts of the world together into one.

Without this love, symbolized by Christmas, people lose their way and fight one another until death. When this love is absent, life gets twisted until people become cynical and bitter. Forget about this love, and self becomes God. Deny it, and cast your lot with demons. Deny it, and you cast your lot with those who believe that someday there will be a final triumph of the demonic. Practice it not, and your name is Scrooge.

The message of Christmas is very simple and yet very profound. The message of Christmas is that God has humbled himself. The message of Christmas is that glory has become simplicity, and simplicity has become glorious. The message of Christmas is that the Word has become flesh. God has become human. Heaven has come down to earth, and eternity has invaded time.

To celebrate a real Christmas is to see hope surfacing in a twisted humanity. It is to see salvation coming through the humble in spirit. It is to truly believe that the wonder of God's love can be and is embodied in flesh.

To believe in a real Christmas is to stake your life and mine on the belief that God has come, not in power, but in innocence, even in the innocence of a baby which means, of course, that God is always easy to turn down. It is hard to know without question about this kind of Christmas, but to know about this kind of Christmas is to know that Heaven is not very far away from earth and that eternity is always present in time.

Recently, I had lunch with a newspaper reporter. Although it is not always a pleasant or easy thing to do, I wanted to speak rather forthrightly to him about the way the religious community is treated in the news today. He wanted to talk to me about the meaning of the Christmas stories. We had planned to meet for lunch for forty-five minutes, but we ate and talked for nearly an hour and a half. As a good newspaper reporter does, he asked pointed questions; and I tried to give him some straight, honest answers.

We talked about the differences in the way the birth stories are pictured in the Bible. Matthew is interested in the genealogy of Jesus. He wants to get it fixed in our minds that Jesus is of the lineage of David, and so he records Jesus' genealogy at the beginning of the Gospel. Luke gives us some details about the birth story including angels, shepherds, cradles, songs, and the people's response to the birth of Christ. This Luke does in a very sensitive and telling way. Mark, on the other hand, doesn't care a thing in the world about the birth stories of Jesus. Mark is interested in the crucifixion, so he says nothing about Christ's birth. John's account of the birth of Christ waxes with eloquent poetry: "In the beginning was the Word and the Word was God, and the Word was with God, and the Word became flesh and dwelt among us, full of grace and full of truth." Saint Paul, however, never mentions the birth of Christ in any of his letters. He never says one word about the birth of Jesus.

We talked about the meanings of these different accounts — the descriptions, the implications, and the beauty in *all* of them. And as we talked, a newspaper reporter — who, of all people, is supposed to be objective, hard, and a bit cynical because he sees the back-end of life so much — looked across the table and said with a quiver in his lip, "Joe, now that we have talked about all of these birth stories, it seems to me that the human mind could not have invented a tale like this."

I believe that this is true — the human mind could not have invented a tale like this because these birth stories are about the Ultimate.

When I was a student at Vanderbilt Divinity School, I was very interested in a theologian by the name of Paul Tillich. I learned in my theology classes that one of the central teachings of Paul Tillich was that whatever our ultimate concern is, this is our "god." If our ultimate concern is money, then money is our "god." If our ultimate concern is our position, then our position is our "god." If our ultimate concern is security, then security is "god." If our ultimate concern is having a good name, then our good name becomes "god." According to Paul Tillich whatever our ultimate concern is, that is "god" for us. Well, I was just full of all this talk as a young seminarian.

One weekend, I went to my little country church down in West Tennessee. I enjoyed talking to a member of that church. His name was Corney Kent. Now, Corney is an awkward name, to say the least. But I used to tell Corney that if I ever had a son, I would name him "Corney"; and both my wife and his wife would say, "I dare you."

Corney was not an educated man but he was a wise man. On Saturday afternoon I would go to the cotton gin to talk to Corney. We would fall into conversation about this and that. I told Corney what Paul Tillich had taught me that week about ultimate concern: whatever our ultimate concern is that is our "god." I waxed eloquent with old Corney as he sat across the room in his cane-bottomed chair. Dressed in his bib overalls with his glasses pulled down on the end of his nose, he chewed on his old corncob pipe and listened very carefully and attentively to me.

After I had finished my little mini-theology lesson with Corney, I turned to him and I said, "Corney, what is your ultimate concern in life?"

He twisted his pipe around between his lips a little bit, moved his glasses back up on his nose, and peered across the room at me, and said, "That the Ultimate is concerned about me."

That is the meaning of Christmas — that the Ultimate is concerned about us. The Ultimate was so concerned about us that he took flesh upon himself and dwelt among us so that we might have a human picture of what God is like. And as the Ultimate is concerned about us, so should we be concerned about each other.

When God's Mind is Spoken

I went to see him at the hospital where he was recuperating from a scary illness. While I visited with him, his wife made arrangements to check him out of the hospital. It took much longer than both of us had expected, so he and I had an unanticipated, but very important, conversation. He worships every Sunday. He never misses Sunday school. He reads my sermons, and those of other ministers, that are mailed to his house. For a lay person, he is theologically well informed. In fact, from time to time, he asks me to give him some titles of books that he can read about Christian theology and Christian ethics. He is a man who seeks to understand the faith and who lives by its implications in this life.

During our visit he made an observation and raised a question. He said, "Pastor, I hear people say that God told them this and God told them that; but, I have never heard God talk. If God ever spoke his mind, what would God say? Anyway, how does one know what is on God's mind?"

I suppose that many people think pastors spend their time responding to questions like this — faith questions. But, I must say that it is rare for a lay person to ask his or her pastor a question that is so centered in faith's reflection. How, then, does one answer the open inquiry of this lay person and the silent questioning of many who say, "Does God speak? And, if so, how?

When we, as human beings, want to share what is on our minds we use words. Our words are expressions of our minds. Every mind must express itself because activity is the very nature of a mind. A mind which is vacant or inactive is not a mind. A mind by its very nature is active, creative, and expressive.

If God ever decided to speak his mind, what would he say and how would he go about saying it? Would God speak his mind with words inscribed on a stone? Or with music? Or with law? Or with a volume containing sixty-six books? If God had something that he really wanted to say to us, how would he choose to say it? And, how could God communicate in a way that we could really understand? Has God ever said what is on his mind? Will God ever say what is on his mind?

The prologue to the Gospel of John tells us about a time when God spoke his mind. These introductory verses tell us that God spoke his mind by becoming flesh and by dwelling among us full of grace and full of truth.

John says that when God wants to speak, God has his Word become flesh. Could there be any higher compliment paid to the human community than to say that God has joined humanity as a person? Dare John say that, in Jesus Christ, God has pitched his tent among us? John is bold in saying that the Word that was with God, and the Word that was God, has now, in the Incarnation, become a living Word. The Word which makes all things now becomes displayed in a human being. The Word which brought forth life and light is now wrapped in human flesh.

From the outset, John wants his reader to understand that when God spoke his mind, he did it not with words, not with another law, but with a person. When God spoke his mind, he did so with Jesus of Nazareth, God's creed for humanity. The teachings, the life, the death, and the resurrection of Jesus Christ best express the mind of God. Thus, Christianity dares to say that the infant Jesus was the expression of the living mind of the living God.

Those who worship here today and in Christian churches everywhere surely know that not all people believe that the Word became flesh in Jesus Christ. Every age has produced its opposition to the Word made flesh. Every age has had its agnostics and skeptics. Every age has had those who have not believed that the Word was made flesh in Jesus Christ. Every age has had those who believe that God does not speak in human form.

John acknowledges that not everyone would believe that the Word had become flesh. He says,

The true light that enlightens every man was coming into the world. He was in the world, and the world was made through him, yet the world knew him not. He came to his own home, and his own people received him not. But to all who received him, who believed in his name, he gave power to become the children of God; who were born, not of blood nor of the will of the flesh nor the will of man, but of God.

Acknowledging that the Word has become flesh is not based upon popular vote. It is not a democratic process. It is not something that is decided by public decree. Instead, there will always be people who cannot accept, or who refuse to accept, the belief that the Word became flesh in Jesus Christ.

However, not all people have disbelieved. The rejection of the Incarnation has never been universal. In every age, there have been a few who believed that God spoke his Word in Jesus Christ. There have always been those who would not disown their belief that the light has overcome the darkness. There have always been those who have seen a unique revelation of God in Jesus Christ.

The decision to believe that God spoke in Jesus Christ is one that each of us has to make. Either we believe that God made a statement in Jesus Christ, or we do not believe it. No one forces us to believe. Not even God stacks the cards against us so that we must believe. The decision to hear what God said through the Incarnation is ours and ours alone. It can never be made for us.

John believed that God had spoken a unique word in Jesus Christ when he wrote, "The Word became flesh." When he wrote this, he did not, of course, mean that the eternal Word became a piece of flesh. What he meant was that the eternal Word became manifest in one who was flesh of our flesh and bone of our bone. A dramatic poet is speaking here — not a dogmatic theologian, nor a speculative philosopher, nor a careful scientist. John does not say that the Word coincided in a special manner with the Jesus of history. He uses hymnic language to say that the eternal, creating, redeeming, sustaining Word of God has now been displayed in a human being.

But, to say that the Word became flesh in Jesus is not to say that God's activity was exhausted by his self-manifestation in Jesus Christ. The presence of God in Jesus does not involve God's absence from the rest of the universe. The grace of God that filled Jesus was not, as a consequence, used up. Let the church understand that God did not cease to speak after he spoke in Jesus Christ.

Throughout history, there have been other people and events through which God disclosed himself to humanity. John says, "We beheld his glory" in Jesus Christ. "Glory" is the manifestation of essential being. "The heavens declare the glory of God," wrote the psalmist. And, whatever awakens us to the reality of the presence of God is a manifestation of divine glory. Tintern Abbey was this for Wordsworth. The Thames was this for Francis Thompson. The "Flower in the Crannied Wall" was this for Tennyson. If we could describe this glory so full of grace and truth, how fitting to say, as John said, that it was the glory of one who knew himself to be as the only son of his father. So uniquely the divine presence dwelled within Jesus! So trustful and so obedient was this fellowship — like that between a father and his only son — that although no one has ever seen God, we can read about Jesus' life, ponder his secret, and say, surely God's presence is here.

Although God is here in the person of Jesus, he is not

exclusively here in the person of Jesus. But, for the Christian, God's Word uniquely became flesh at the Incarnation.

So I said to my friend in the hospital, "If you want to hear the Word of God, listen to it drummed out in the life of Jesus, because it is in the earthly life of Jesus that one can hear God's eternal Word."

I had an old history teacher in college who was somewhat agnostic. He certainly did not hold to orthodox theology. He did not believe in the historic creeds of Christianity. He said they were a bunch of words put together by high-flying thinkers. He was unsure about many doctrinal statements relating to God, Jesus, and the Holy Spirit. He often spoke about his doubts. He would have sympathized with Tennyson's words — "There lives more faith in honest doubt, believe me, than in half the creeds." This crusty old teacher would often share his doubts with us — doubts drawn from long years of trying to understand the meaning of life and its historical underpinnings.

At that time in my life, I was trying to decide whether I should be a historian or a pastor. I loved history. I enjoyed studying it, and I wanted to teach it. Late one afternoon I went to my professor's office and asked him to help me think through this question of my vocation. I shared with him my love for history and my calling to be a minister in the church. After listening very intently to me, he said, "I want you to leave my office considering the possibility that Jesus of Nazareth is the best human picture that we have of God. If Jesus is the best picture we have of God, then what implications does that have for your life."

In his own unorthodox way my history teacher invited me to listen anew to the Word made flesh. This listening is not a once-and-for-all kind of listening. It is the kind of listening that must take place over and over again, day in and day out, if we are to continue to hear the shaping Word of God in our midst.

A group of college students had a faith discussion. They

said, among other things, "We think that we have Confirmation class too early in the United Methodist Church. We wish we had had our Confirmation when we were at least in Junior High School, if not in the ninth grade. We have forgotten a lot of what we'd learned about the faith. We are not sure what we believe or why we believe it."

To be sure, the church may have failed its youth. To be sure, we may not have taught the faith concisely and clearly. But there might just be another side to that coin; and that other side might be that those youth, like a lot of us, have quit listening to the Word that became flesh.

Listening to the Word made flesh must always be voluntary if it is to do any good. On the whole, people do not attain strong spirituality out of a sense of duty. We cannot compel others to listen to the Word made flesh; nor can we be compelled. Being shaped by the Word made flesh depends upon a pull more than a push. We cannot be pushed into hearing the word that God has spoken in Christ. Cheap scolding will not cause others to listen. Nor will cheap scolding cause us to listen. If we listen, it will be because we hunger to hear what God said when God spoke in Jesus Christ.

Said John, "No one has ever seen God. The Word made flesh has made him known." I say to you and to myself — *Listen. Listen. Listen.* A church that fails to listen to the Word made flesh becomes like a ship without a rudder. A life that refuses to listen to the Word made flesh becomes like a car without a steering wheel. A family that refuses to listen to the Word made flesh listens only to the voices of culture that pound and beat against it.

Listen. God has spoken clearly, and God has spoken in a way that all can understand. God spoke by coming as a person — Jesus of Nazareth.

Responding to Christ's Birth

Telling the story of Christ's birth was not enough for Matthew! He also told about two reactions to the birth of the Messiah.

The first reaction, as Matthew told it, was from the Magi who came from the East to Jerusalem and asked the question, "Where is the newborn king of the Jews?" Contemporary customs — children dressed in faded bathrobes, tired Christmas pageants, and unsightly stable scenes in church parking lots, have taken away from the wisdom of the Wise Men's story.

It is difficult to understand what Matthew meant by *Magi*. They might have been Zoroastrian priests who had special power to interpret dreams. Or, they could have been men who practiced various forms of secret love and magic. In the Old Testament, they were referred to as enchanters, astronomers, and interpreters of dreams and of visionary messages. In early first-century Rome, they were known as astrologers, magicians, and readers of dreams. In Acts 8:9-24, Luke tells the story of Simon, a magus and false prophet on the island of Cyprus. Therefore, the term *magi* refers to a large number of people engaged in occult arts. It covers a wide range of astronomers, fortune-tellers, priestly augurs, and wandering magicians. Since Matthew depicted the Magi as having seen a star, it is highly possible that they were astrologers from beyond Palestine.

In the Old Testament the "people of the East" were also desert Arabs. These nomadic Arabs often had wise men as a natural part of their envoy. Proverbs 30:1, Proverbs 31:1, and 1 Kings 5:12 refer to the wisdom that was commonly associated with these wise men. Likewise, astrology was not unknown to the Arabs. Arabian tribes often took their names from the stars. In addition, gold, frankincense, and myrrh were gifts that eastern Arabs would use to express their feelings.

According to Matthew, these Arab astrologers reacted to the birth of Jesus by following a star to the city of Jerusalem, a scant five miles from the hill town of Bethlehem. After inquiring about the birthplace of Jesus, they followed the star to Bethlehem where they found the child and Mary, his mother. Having found the infant, they bowed down and paid him homage. Then they opened their treasure boxes and brought out gifts of gold, frankincense, and myrrh.

For centuries, people have speculated about the meaning of these gifts. In each special gift, there is rich symbolism and deep meaning, for in each, one sees the wisdom of the Magi. Thankfully, the Arab astrologers did not bring the child a toy, a silver spoon, or a teething ring. Nor did they bring a cute little outfit for his circumcision. Nor did they bring clothing or flowers for his mother. Instead, they brought gifts that expressed their hope for the Christ child.

One of the treasure boxes contained gold, the king of metals, because the Wise Men wanted Jesus to be the "King of Kings." An ancient writer Seneca said that one should never approach a king without the gift of gold. So the gift of gold was presented because the astrologers wanted Bethlehem's babe to become the Lord of life.

Jesus' life, as we know, did not unfold like many had expected. In fact, Jesus was a complete reversal of what the world had expected from its kings. He ruled not with power, but with love. Self-surrender and service were his methods. He became the friend of hated tax collectors, flagrant sinners, the forgotten poor, and the misunderstood outcast. The gift of gold should serve as a constant reminder to us that we have been identified by God whose power is rooted in love and self-surrender. Frankincense, an aromatic gum resin used for incense by priests, was brought as the second gift. There is the possibility that these traveling Wise Men wanted the baby to become a priest. The chief role of a priest is to build bridges between God and people. The Wise Men wanted the Son of God to be the bridge which would connect God to all people and all people to each other.

The New Testament speaks about Jesus as one who spent his life building bridges, not barriers. Those who are marked as his followers are also called to be priests and to build bridges for each other. The church, by its very essence, is called to build bridges, between black and white, the rich and poor, the Western centers of power and the Third World, the "haves" and the "have nots" — wherever separations appear in the life of humanity. The church that does not bring people together in community is simply not a church of Jesus Christ. The will of God is done when people are fashioned into communities of mutual love and respect.

The third gift box contained myrrh, used in the ancient world to embalm the dead. It is a symbol of suffering. These Gentile astrologers wanted their Messiah to be the kind of Lord who would suffer for his people. They did not want a Christ who would dodge a cross, would be protected from the hurts of humanity, or would fail to identify with the lonely and alienated. They wanted a Saviour who would suffer for and would take upon himself the sufferings of humanity.

According to the Gospels, Jesus lived up to the suffering symbolized by myrrh through the glory of his passion, death, and resurrection. The real church, the genuine community of believers, exists wherever and whenever people of faith enter into the sufferings of humanity as Jesus did.

These gifts could also be symbols relating to the different aspects of the Christian response to the Messiah's birth: gold symbolizes virtue, frankincense symbolizes prayer, and myrrh symbolizes suffering.

Believers do not respond to the birth of the Christ child in a vacuum, nor do they respond with an overdose of ceremony, with empty words, or with false deeds. Most Christians react to Christ's birth by displaying a life full of good deeds. "By this my Father is glorified," said Jesus, "that you bear much fruit." (John 15:8) Not to bear good fruit is to be distant from the spirit of the living Christ. Good deeds are indeed the gold of Christian life.

Nor can Christians be fed for their journey without prayer. Prayer is that resource which helps us to practice the presence of Christ in every relationship of our lives. Rufus M. Jones, in *The Double Search*, puts it this way:

> *It is a primary truth of Christianity that God reaches us directly. No person is insulated. As oceans flood the inlets, as sunlight environs the plant, so God enfolds and enwreathes the finite spirit. There is this difference, however, inlet and plant are penetrated whether they will or not. Sea and sunshine crowd themselves in a tergo. Not so with God. He can be received only through doors that are purposely opened for him. A person may live as near God as the bubble is to the ocean and yet not find him. He may be "closer than breathing, nearer than hands or feet," and still be missed. Historically Christianity is dry and formal when it lacks the immediate and inward response to our Great Companion; but our spirits are trained to know him, to appreciate him, by the mediation of historical revelation. A person's spiritual life is always dwarfed when cut away from history. Mysticism is empty unless it is enriched by outward and historical revelation. The supreme education of the soul comes through an intimate acquaintance with the Jesus Christ of history.*

Likewise, the symbol of myrrh continues to call Christians to live a life of passion. Today it appears that passion for life itself is disappearing. Many fear that the world will end in atomic death. Others expect ecological death. It seems that we will come to ruin long before that by means of our own apathy. Too many of us have gotten used to life. As we have become accustomed to crime in our large cities, so we have become accustomed to the threat of death through nuclear weapons and through the destruction of our environment. We have become accustomed to death even before it comes. Why? Because when the passionate devotion to life is missing, the powers to resist evil are paralyzed. Therefore, if we want to live today, we must consciously will life. We must learn to love life with such a passion that we no longer become accustomed to the powers of destruction. We must overcome our own apathy and be seized by the passion for life.

To follow as a disciple means to share in both the joy and the suffering of humanity. Christ's people are concerned about the joy and the hurt of life, but neither one to the exclusion of the other. Good news and passion are linked together in this faith. There can be no Gospel without passion. As we travel in "The Way", we gradually understand that the Gospel, as symbolized by myrrh, must have passion as well as success.

Matthew wanted to convey that some reacted to the birth of Jesus with acceptance and devotion. He did this by showing that the first to pay homage to the newborn King of the Jews were Gentiles from the East. In these Magi, Matthew anticipated all of those who would respond to Christ's birth by paying homage.

Woven into this touching story of the Magi's devotion is the parable of Herod's reaction to the birth of the King of the Jews. Herod responded to the birth not by paying homage, but by plotting to kill the child. Therein lies a paradox: Herod, the chief priests, and the scribes — people who have read the Scriptures and could plainly see what the prophets have said — were not willing to worship the newborn king. Thus, we have a two-fold reaction to the birth of Christ. The Wise Men of the Gentiles accepted and paid homage, but the ruler of Jerusalem and all the chief priests and scribes of the people do not believe. Rather, they conspired against the King of the Jews and sought his death.

It is not difficult to understand why Herod responded as

he did. His kingdom was threatened by the possibility of a new king. The possibility of being displaced did not bring him great joy. Instead, it brought fear. If this child was truly the Messiah, it would alter all that Herod believed to be important.

In *The Gospel in Solentiname*, Ernesto Cardenal reports that after reading Matthew 2, a Nicaraguan farm worker responded by saying: "I think these wise men [fouled] things up when they went to Herod asking about a liberator. It would be like someone going to Somoza now to ask him where's the man who is going to liberate Nicaragua."

Whenever and wherever the message of Christ is taken into the world, there is the possibility that it will be met with rejection.

I was a pastor in Memphis, Tennessee, when Dr. Martin Luther King, Jr., was shot while he stood on the balcony of a downtown motel. I learned of the shooting when our black custodian interrupted the Finance Committee meeting by shouting, "Dr. King has been shot! Dr. King has been shot!" The next morning's issue of *The Commerical Appeal*, our local newspaper, urgently called the clergy of the city to a meeting.

Pastors representing every racial, cultural, and educational group in the city gathered for the mass meeting which had been called for by the bold headlines of the city newspaper. The Reverend James Lawson, a friend of Dr. King's and an effective pastor in South Memphis, read the Old Testament lesson. The local Greek Orthodox priest read from the New Testament and symbolically kissed the feet of Mr. Lawson. The Reverend Frank McRae, a courageous leader in the United Methodist Church, spoke about hope in the midst of despair.

After a time of Bible study, prayer, and speaking, the clergy decided to march *en masse* to the office of Mayor Henry Loeb, as a symbol of love and reconciliation. We wanted the Mayor to reconsider his opposition to the striking sanitation workers as a symbol of repentance and love.

After leaving the sanctuary, we formed ourselves in lines, two abreast, and started walking toward the City Hall. Just before we had completed one block of our march, a young deacon from St. Mary's ran back into the church and brought out the processional cross commonly used on Sunday morning for the worship service. With humility and yet boldness, he put himself at the head of the processional, now aimed at the city's seat of power. As we walked, television cameras descended upon us. Reporters from New York to California started pumping us with questions about our motives and about how we felt about what had happened the night before.

When our journey was about half completed, an older woman started yelling from a second floor apartment window. Because of the traffic, the cameras, and the reporters, her speech was at first inaudible. As I drew closer to her flowerbox window, I could hear the anger of her shrill voice: "The cross belongs in the church! The cross belongs in the church! I am a member of St. Mary's. Take the cross back to the church where it belongs." Her secure kingdom, like Herod's, had been threatened; and, she responded not with homage, but with rejection.

The message of Jesus often brings peace, but it also brings trouble. Even in our contemporary society, Christ's message of love, justice, and peace invades our kingdoms of selfishness, pride, power, injustice, and provincialism. The Herods continue to stalk the world and try to discover ways to silence the message. In our modern world, there are evil forces which tirelessly attempt to silence the message of Christ.

Those who have responded to the revelation of God in Christ instinctively know that rejection is possible. As H. Richard Niebuhr notes in *The Meaning of Revelation*:

When we speak of revelation . . . we mean rather that something has happened which compels our faith and which requires us to seek rationality and unity in the whole of our history. Revelation is like the Kingdom of God not only by its immediate worth but also by its instrumental value in leading to secondary goods, and revelation proves itself to be revelation of reality not only by its intrinsic verity, but also by its ability to guide people to many other truths.

Disciples of Jesus, having been led to "many other truths," can expect both affirmation and rejection.

Therefore, there are two reactions to the appearance of the Messiah: homage and rejection. It is too easy and clean to say that some respond by giving, as did the Magi, while others react by opposing the meaning of Christ's birth, as did Herod. Not one person reading these words is entirely like the Magi. Nor is he or she exactly like Herod. We are, at best, a mixture of devotion and denial. We are neither one nor the other, but an uneasy mixture of both.

Many country music artists understand the dual nature that exists within humankind. While on stage, the country musician can sing about sex, lust, cheating, gambling, and unfaithfulness and, then, close the program by singing "Amazing Grace". The contradiction is shockingly apparent, but so typical of how we really are.

What happens on the country music stage is a microcosm of what much of our lives are like. For six days every week, we live sinful, broken lives and then sing the hymns of faith with great feeling on the following Sunday morning. In spite of the hell we have created or have been through, we flock to Christmas Eve services with faith welling up within us. In spite of the alienation and despair we either cause or experience, we insist upon attaching ourselves to the community of believers.

Frederick Buechner says in *Telling The Truth*:

> *Joy happens, to use Tolkien's word, and the fairy tale where it happens is not a world where everything is sweetness and light. It is not Disney Land where everything is kept spotless . . . On the contrary, the world where this joy happens is as full of darkness as our own world, and that is why when it happens it is as poignant as grief and can bring tears to our eyes. It can bring tears to our eyes because it might so easily not have happened.*

Today marks the first Sunday after Christmas, often the

most undervalued celebration of the Christian year. It is this day that proclaims the purpose of the Incarnation: the manifestation of God through Christ to the world. As Chrysotom preached in A.D. 386, "Up to this day he [Jesus] was unknown to the multitudes." In this season of manifestation, we are drawn to understand God as revealed to both the Herods and the Gentile Arab astrologers. The revelation of God is up to God, not us. But, one of the things that makes this such a day of unbridled celebration is precisely the nature of God. It is God's nature to come to us, to search us out, to meet us on the journey, and to make himself known to us. It is God's nature not to be known by a few people, but by the multitudes. God yearns to be known. God is an encountering God, and that is the reason the Wise Men found Jesus. They responded, and they were led where they were beckoned. They were willing to look for the king in unlikely places. What they found was a surprise. Expecting to find the future king, they encountered a living God.

Having experienced the living God, they returned home by a different route. If we have really experienced God during these days of Christmas, then we will return home as different people who travel by a different way.

Submission

Pete Maravich and Lily Laskin had something in common aside from the fact that they both died one day apart. They both gave themselves to that which they considered important.

People who keep up with harps and harpists say that Lily Laskin, the French harpist, took the harp out of the living room and made it a featured solo instrument on concert stages all over the world. She died on January 4, 1988, at the age of ninety-four. Upon her death, she was credited with popularizing the harp and reviving many musical scores written for it by such composers as Handel and Camille Saint-Seans. She started playing the harp as a child and continued giving public performance well into her eighties. At the age of sixteen, she became the first woman harpist at the Paris Opera. Best known for her interpretation of Mozart she gave a landmark performance of his concerto for flute and harp, at the Salzburg Music Festival in 1937. She recorded it many times during the years, along with works by Maurice Ravel and Claude Debussy.

Pete Maravich, the outstanding basketball player of modern times, died on January 5, 1988. While at LSU, he averaged forty-four points per game. No one defensive system in the Southeastern Conference could stop him. Some coaches devised complicated double-team defenses to shut him down. Others let him shoot at will and put pressure on the other four players. As a professional player, Maravich consistently

66

knocked the bottom out of the basket. His dazzling perfor-
mances sold tickets for big bucks. Host teams could be assured
of a sell-out game when "Pistol Pete" came to town. Ironi-
cally, Maravich died at the age of forty just after playing a
pick-up game at a local church gym.

Both Lily Laskin and Pete Maravich gave themselves to
that which they considered important. She was totally submitted to the harp, and he was in subjection of basketball. Lily
once said, "I have built my life around the harp." On many
occasions Pete observed, "Basketball is my whole life."

In one way or another all of us submit ourselves to that
which is important to us. One night a few years ago, Vanderbilt played basketball at Memorial Gym. Although there was
four inches of snow on the ground, it came as no surprise to
anyone that the gym was not empty. Sport fans hired cabs,
rode buses, drove automobiles, and tramped through bitter
cold temperatures to watch the game. Basketball was so important to so many fans that nothing could stymie their efforts to see the game.

For some, work is the most important thing; all that we
are revolves around it. Without work many have no identity.
What a person does becomes what a person "is". For others,
relationships are the most important thing. To have the benevo-
lence, love, and friendship of others can become an all con-
suming passion of life. Many of our brothers and sisters believe
that pleasure is the most important thing. Life is centered in
having a good time. Those who rank pleasure at the top of
the list believe that happiness is the result of pleasure. Others
are compelled by the forces of life to feel that the preserva-
tion of life is the most important thing. "Today," said Paul
Tillich, "the simple concern for food and clothing and shelter
is so overwhelming in the greater part of mankind that it has
almost suppressed most of the other human concerns, and it
has absorbed the minds of all classes of people." (*The New
Being*, p. 155)

Am I not correct in saying that what we give ourselves to

is the most important thing to us? Can anyone deny that? The question is not, "Will we submit ourselves to what we consider to be the most important thing?" The primary question is, "What is the most important thing to which we can submit ourselves?"

In writing about the baptism of Jesus, Matthew speaks on the latter question. When Jesus came to John the Baptizer to be baptized, John tried to prevent him saying, "I need to be baptized by you, and do you come to me?" Jesus then told John why he had come to be baptized. He did not say that he had come for baptism for the remission of sin. Nor did he say that he had come because John was more or less worthy. Jesus said that he had come to "fulfill all righteousness."

Jesus was saying that he had come to be baptized in order to fulfill the commands of God. For Matthew, a person who "fulfills all righteousness" is one who is totally submitted to God's authority. Thus, baptism for Jesus was an act of fidelity to God. Baptism was Jesus' statement that submission to God's authority would be the most important thing in his life. God, according to Matthew, was pleased with the obedience of Jesus. So pleased was God that the heavens opened, and the Spirit of God descended like a dove while a voice from Heaven said, "This is my beloved Son with whom I am well pleased."

This Sunday we observe the Baptism of the Lord. It is not a big feast day of the church, like All Saints Day or Christmas. It is certainly not a "little Easter." It is a Sunday when we reflect upon the baptism of Jesus. It is a time when we remember how Jesus submitted himself to God's authority, and how he lived out that authority in every aspect of his life and teachings. It is also a time for us to remember how living under God's authority took him to a cross and to the Resurrection.

But, this Sunday is more than a time for us to reflect and remember. It is more than a time for us to recall how Jesus, through his baptism, submitted himself to God's authority and, therefore, identified himself with sinful humanity. This day was written into the church calendar so that we would not forget that we have followed the example of our Lord. Through baptism, we have submitted ourselves to God's authority. Like Jesus, we have been baptized. Like our Lord, we have given ourselves to God's reign in our lives. We are thereby marked as Christ's disciples and initiated into Christ's Holy Church. Through baptism, we have been ordained to our ministry in the world.

If I were building a new church, I would put the baptismal font or pool in a prominent place near the front door of the nave. I would want every worshiper to be confronted by it every Sunday morning. I would want worshipers to walk around it before getting to a pew. I would want those who come and go from the church to do so with the persistent and constant reminder that they have been baptized.

The baptismal font in our sanctuary stands just to the east of the pulpit. It stands before us and in our midst as we worship God. As with all baptismal fonts that are properly built, this one has eight sides representing the eight days of Creation. Thus, in baptism, we are made a part of the new creation. This font, standing where it does, will not let us forget that we have been initiated into this congregation, as well as into the universal church. It reminds us that we have been grafted as a member of the Body of Christ — marked and identified as a Christian disciple. It will not let us erase from our memory that we have been born anew in the water and in the Spirit.

Let us not forget that baptism is as much a rite of passage for the church as it is for the person being baptized. When a new person joins the Body of Christ, neither the member nor the church will ever be the same again. During baptism, the church commits itself to the nurturing of its new member — through worship, church school classes and other nurturing groups, pastoral care, and the ongoing love and concern of other members — regardless of whether the one baptized is an infant or a mature adult.

Likewise, every time a person is baptized in our congregation, it should remind us of the importance of renewing the vows which we made, or which were made for us, at our baptism. Let every baptism which takes place in our congregation speak to us about the importance of submitting ourselves anew to God's authority in our lives.

Submission is a notion which does not sit well with contemporary people. The assertion of one's rights establishes the mood of our day. Freedom from authority is the banner that is hoisted by the masses. To be "laid back" is a virtue. We do not want anyone or anything to have power over our lives. Yet, baptism is about submission. It is about being joined to Christ.

Submission through baptism does not enslave us. Rather, it sets us free. The more we submit to Christ, the freer we are to live joyful lives of love and service. When giving ourselves to Christ becomes the most important consideration, we are made free to respond to the hurts and hopes of God's people, whoever they are and whenever they cross our path.

Pete Maravich was free to play the game because he was totally submitted to what the game required of him. Lily Laskin was free to play the harp because she was committed to what it took to be a great harpist. Christians who are free to love and serve are first and foremost submitted to God's authority in all of life.

Earlier in this worship service, I gave the Sacrament of Baptism to John Edward Fitzpatrick. When I asked, "What name is this child given?", his mother and father said, "John Edward." He was named for his grandfathers, both of whom are now deceased. After taking John Edward into my arms, I baptized him in the name of the Father, Son, and Holy Spirit. I hope the day will come when he will take the faith for himself and be confirmed as a member of Christ's Universal Church. It is our hope and prayer that his life will be submitted to God's authority — that he will live out the meaning of his baptism.

John Edward now lives his life as a person who has been baptized. That mark is on him. He may not choose to live by the meaning of baptism, but he can never erase what has happened today. He will pass through the innocence of childhood as a baptized person. He will handle the peer pressure of adolescence as a baptized youngster. As a mature adult, he will make moral and ethical decisions as one who has been baptized. He will face old age as one who has been joined to the Body of Christ. He will make love, fill out his income tax, and decide what to give away and what to keep as one of Christ's people. He will make up his mind about issues like war, sexuality, affluence, and relations as one on whom the water has been sprinkled.

He has been baptized. And, so have we.

The Bodily
Glorification of God

Glorify God with your body. Glorify God with your body. Glorify God with your body.

What did Saint Paul mean when he said, "Glorify God with your body"? I suppose Saint Paul had a lot of time to think about things like that because, after all, Saint Paul spent a lot of time in jail. When you spend a lot of time in jail, you have some time to think about some things like glorifying God with your body.

This is hard for us to hear because we know how to glorify the body, but we do not know how to glorify God with the body.

I say to you that we know how to glorify the body. Last night, I went shopping with Janene, my wife, and I bought one of these new little boxes that can be used to store things in closets. You can stack them, roll them, push them, and turn them upside down. When I put that little webbed box in my closet, I happened to look at all my clothing — trousers, shirts, suits, sport coats, and topcoats. Most of my clothing is there, not because I need it, but because I need it to glorify my body. It is there to make me look good before others and to help me feel good about myself.

A lot of the physical fitness craze today is not as much about physical fitness as it is about glorifying the body.

71

Joggers pound the street. There is a plethora of work-out books. Why, you can even buy records and videos that tell you how to turn flab into firmness and fat into muscle. To be sure, it is important to stay in shape, but much of this craze is just to glorify the body.

Four symbols illustrate our obsession with glorifying the body. The first symbol is heard in the phrase "Dress to win!" Learn how to dress so you can be a winner. The worst thing you could ever do is to show up dressed in the wrong clothing. When the ties get narrow, don't wear a wide one. When the shirts get shorter, don't wear a long one. You have to know how to dress to win, that is how to glorify the body.

The second symbol is the tanning spa. People are paying what I consider to be a very high price to tan their bodies so their bodies can be glorified. Now, all of us know that tanning spas are not good for you. Some are even saying they can permanently damage one's skin. Yet, because we are so obsessed with glorifying the body, we will pay high prices to get brown, even though this is not good for us.

The third symbol is *Playboy* and *Playgirl* magazines where the human body is exalted as an object of sexual gratification.

The fourth symbol is steroids. People take steroids to distort the muscles of the body in order to be a better athlete. When one pumps iron after taking steroids, the muscles in the body take on added dimension and strength.

So I say to you, we know a lot about how to glorify the body, but we don't know very much about how to glorify God with the body.

One of the reasons we don't know how to glorify God with the body is that we have been taught to glorify God with our spirits, but not with our bodies. We have been taught that the body is not as important as the spirit. We have been taught that spiritual glorification is more important than physical glorification.

The New Testament was written at a time heavily influenced by the Greeks. Many of the thoughts in the New Testament are there because the New Testament writers picked up those of the Greek world around them. One of the fundamental teachings of the Greek culture was that the body is simply a crate for the soul. Those who wrote the New Testament picked up on this and said, therefore, the spirit is really more important than the body. So we have been taught down through the centuries to glorify God with our spirits and to discount our bodies.

But Apostle Paul tried to correct that notion when he said, "Glorify God with the body. Glorify God with the body!"

How is it then that we glorify God with the body? Saint Paul said we glorify God with the body by shunning immorality.

In Corinth, there was a big temple that had as many as five hundred prostitutes. The men of Corinth and the sailors who came across the isthmus often warmed themselves with booze and slid under the covers with a prostitute. This was not unlawful, but according to Saint Paul, this was immoral. So, Saint Paul said that we glorify God with the body by shunning immorality. To "shun" immorality means don't flirt with temptation. When our Lord taught us to pray, he taught us to pray so that we would not be led into temptation.

Furthermore, Saint Paul said that the body is not meant for immorality, but for the Lord and the Lord for the body. The body, in other words, is a member of Christ's body. According to Paul's *strong* imagery, when a person goes to the temple and joins himself to a prostitute, that person and that prostitute become one. And so it is, said Saint Paul, that our bodies are joined to Christ. Therefore, we glorify God with our bodies when we remember that the body is the temple of the Holy Spirit. The physical body is a sacred thing. The human body is not a slab of meat. The human body is not property to be used for display or to be exploited. But, the human body, mine and yours, is sacred in that it is a member of Christ.

Finally, we glorify God with the body when we physically

do things that glorify God. Or, in other words, we glorify God
with the body when we allow our bodies to be used in service
to humankind. This is probably the greatest glorification of
God with the body.

I remember the night I worshiped God at Ebenezer Baptist Church in Atlanta, Georgia. The occasion was the celebration of Dr. Martin Luther King, Jr.'s birthday. Although we
had arrived there very early, we found only a few seats way
up in the balcony. The church was packed with people from
all over the United States — black and white, rich and poor,
people who had been in the streets in the sixties, and people
who felt guilty because they had done nothing in the sixties.
Dr. William Sloane Coffin, the recent pastor of Riverside
Church in New York City, was the preacher. The choir from
Clark College sang. A predominantly white choir from a nearby
Baptist Church provided an anthem. The Ebenezer choir sang
two anthems which stirred the soul.

As I sat there and worshiped God with that great mixture
of people, this thought crossed my mind: These people, meeting in this one Baptist Church, were the cradle of the Civil
Rights movement back then. These people had put it on the
line. They had bodily displayed what they believed. They hadn't
just sat around in the church and talked about peace, justice,
and brotherhood. Instead, they had been physical with it. They
had taken their bodies out into the street where no one could
misunderstand what they stood for.

Maybe that is what Saint Paul meant when he said,
"Glorify God with your body." Maybe he meant, "Quit sitting around *talking* about it and *be* there. *Go* there and put
it on the line."

In a few weeks, people of this church are going on a mission to St. Vincent. They are going to *bodily* witness their faith
in Jesus Christ and their faith in his power to heal and to set
people free. It is one thing to sit in church and think about
witnessing or to sit in a committee and reflect on it, but it is
another thing to do it bodily.

Sometimes, we hear about a death in the family. Or, we hear about someone who is hurting a great deal. If we cross the path of that person, we may say to them, "Just wanted you to know that I've been thinking about you." Now, we know that is not enough. There is a difference between going to that person, wrapping that person in your arms, and being there with her or him and between simply passing them by in the hallway and saying, "I have been thinking about you."

It is bodily involvement in Christianity that really matters. The wonderful thing is that anybody can glorify God with the body. Chubby people, skinny people, distorted people, handicapped people, people like me who have to have a pair of trousers almost remade every time I buy them — any kind of body can glorify God. The culture in which we live says that only beautiful bodies are worth anything: our faith says that everybody's body can glorify God.

Today's Gospel reading tells us how John the Baptizer clarified the identity of Jesus. During the Baptism of Jesus, John the Baptizer saw the Spirit descend upon Jesus in the form of a dove. As the dove descended, God spoke to John and said, "He on whom you see the Spirit descend and remain, this is he who baptizes the Holy Spirit. And I have seen and borne witness that this is the Son of God."

Jesus then left the river Jordan to begin his public ministry. From the murky Jordan to the place called "The Skull," Jesus glorified God not only with his words, but with his flesh-and-blood body. Had it not been for Jesus' bodily glorification of God, God's words about a descending Spirit would have been hollow. It was Jesus' bodily glorification of God which gave validity to the Spirit's work.

So if the Spirit is truly with us, we will glorify God not only with our words, but with our physical bodies as well. "Glorify God with your body," said St. Paul. That's what Jesus did and so should we. How else will the world believe that the Spirit has descended on us?

The Called Ones

The Gospel lesson for today makes me want to fuss at Jesus. It makes me want to fuss at Jesus because the message of the text is so radical! It is radical to believe that people would actually leave their place of business to follow after a teacher who said, "Follow me, and I will make you fishers of men."

After Jesus had finished preaching a sermon in Capernaum, he took a stroll along the banks of the Sea of Galilee. As Jesus walked by the sea side, he noticed two brothers — Simon, who is called Peter, and Andrew, his brother — casting a net into the sea. He called out to them, "Follow me, and I will make you fishers of men." Peter and Andrew did not sit in the boat and reflect on what Jesus said to them. Apparently, they did not count the cost. Nor did they call a committee meeting. Nor did they form an association to provide them with support. Instead, they immediately left their nets and followed him.

As Jesus continued his walk along the sea side, he saw two other brothers — James, the son of Zebedee, and John, his brother, in the boat and Zebedee, their father. They were rocking back and forth in the boat, minding their own business, and mending their nets when Jesus called out to them to follow. As with Peter and Andrew, they left their trade and their father and followed after Jesus of Nazareth. According to Matthew, they did not hesitate. They followed immediately.

Who among us would respond in this way? I mean, how

77

many people in this congregation today would put a padlock on their business and chase a person like Jesus?

I, for one, would argue with Jesus about that. I have a wife and two daughters who need my support. I have house notes, car notes, and bills to pay. I have groceries to buy and clothing to purchase. I have responsibilities to this congregation and to this community. I am involved in many things which are important to me. In a few short months, my younger daughter will be graduating from high school. I want to be there for the baccalaureate, the graduation exercises, the gifts, the parties, and all the rest. Next year, my older daughter will be graduating from Lambuth College. "All the king's horses and all the king's men" could not keep me from being on the Lambuth campus for that special day in the history of our family.

What if everybody followed the example of those fishermen? What if everybody heard the call and heeded it? Who would mind the store? Who would pay the taxes? Who would run the church? Who would paint, make music, or govern? Our tendency is to brush off this story as being unrealistic. After all, not one person in this congregation is going to respond as Peter, Andrew, James, and John did. It is okay for them to be radical in their response. But, it is not okay for us.

On the other hand, one cannot read the New Testament without seeing that some followed in a radical way. Jesus said, "Follow me," to a tax collector named Matthew; and Matthew got up and followed him. Philip, who was from Andrew and Peter's hometown, followed his calling by helping Jesus to feed the five thousand. John reports that Jesus said, "Follow me," and Nathaniel, also known as Bartholomew, followed. According to church tradition, Bartholomew followed the call by carrying the Gospel to various countries, including India. Thomas, having been called, said to his fellow disciples, "Let us also go, that we may die with him." And Paul, who heard Jesus say, "Rise and enter the city and you will be told what to do," went forth and proclaimed: "Jesus is the Son of God."

Every now and then, someone does respond in a radical and unexpected way. Dr. Fred Craddock tells the story of a medical student who heard the call and made a radical response. A young woman came to him after hearing his sermon on today's text. She had decided to leave medical school and go to work among migrant workers in the Rio Grande Valley. Dr. Craddock did not manipulate her unexpected response. Instead, they talked for a long time about the meaning of her decision. Her parents were, understandably, furious with the new direction her life had taken. Like those fishermen, however, she heard the call and she stayed with it.

And there have been others. People in the western tradition have long known about Francis of Assisi. He turned from a life of luxury to one of voluntary poverty with the intention of sharing his possessions with the poor. He became an example to his fellow townspeople of the biblical assurance that God can provide. Francis attracted others to his way of life and began the Order of Mendicant Friars. A sister order was established by Clare, to whom Franics was both friend and mentor. In the hymn of praise attributed to Francis, God is exalted for creating all of the elements of the world of which, according to Francis, humans are only one part. Francis placed people in the perspective of God's whole creation and asserted a relationship of kinship among all the elements. The example of his impoverished life drew others to him, and increased the numbers of the Franciscan Order. His began the first of the monastic groups to develop a spiritual life — a life lived as much in the world as it was in the withdrawn quite life.

Likewise, Elizabeth Gurney Fry (1780-1845) exemplified an emphasis on living by Jesus' example. In addition to raising a large family, this wife of a wealthy London merchant single-handedly initiated, and caused the implementation of, efforts to reform the prison system in England. These reforms spread throughout the continent even during her lifetime.

Similarly, in the United States, Dorothea Lynde Dix (1802-1887) spearheaded the movement for the establishment of hospitals for the mentally ill, who were, at the time, being held in prisons. These people have admonished us to see Christ in our neighbors and to serve all who are in need. In these people and in many others, we see an example of people "leaving their nets" to follow.

I know of a business person who sold his automobile dealership in order to attend a theological seminary in preparation for ordained ministry in the United Methodist Church. I recently heard his wife say, "My husband came home one day and said, 'You will be very surprised at what I am about to say, but I want to sell the business and go into the ministry'!" Within a few days, the business had been sold, and the family began tramping along another path. "We have never been happier," said his wife. There was, for this family, a call and a response. Life, for them, has been reoriented.

During a seminar, a pastor said to me, "I think that I am hearing God call me out of the ordained ministry to the ministry of the laity. Is it possible for God to call me out of the ministry if God, once upon a time, called me into the ministry?" This pastor is beginning to hear a call which demands a response.

It is true that God calls us to journey. But, we do not know what experiences will be found along the path. Don Quixote went on such a journey. His creator, Miguel de Cervantes, was writing a not-so-gentle satire of how people viewed such a journey. John Bunyan's "Christian" went on a journey in *Pilgrim's Progress*. Through temptations and unhappy experiences, Christian stands steadfast in his faith until crossing through the waters of Jordon into the Celestial City. The people of Israel were on a similar journey from Egypt to their promised land. Their faith was sometimes tried and found wanting; but their leader, Moses, was steadfast and so was his appointed successor, Joshua. Likewise, Christians view life as following — following in the steps of Jesus.

Where does that leave us? If others have heard the call and have responded in a radical way, then shouldn't we all do the same? I cannot answer that question for you. It has to be answered by each of us as we experience God's call in our lives. How one hears the call and responds to it is a matter of personal decision.

However, there is an inescapable truth in the story of Jesus' call to the fishermen and their response. The truth is that who we worship can and will make a claim on all of our lives. It is impossible to worship the God of Jesus Christ and not have that God expect more of us than we are often ready to give. Whether or not we respond to the call, the call of Christ is always unsettling. Hearing it is always disturbing. It disrupts our lives and pulls us in new directions.

To heed Christ's call to be a disciple is to follow Jesus, who manifests the kingly authority of God. It means submitting to his authority and turning our lives toward the Kingdom. It means a basic reorientation, from daily chores and activities, to a life oriented toward Christ. It means to direct our lives in a specific direction — the very direction in which Jesus oriented his life. The proclamation of the kingdom is an implicit call to follow Jesus. Thus, being a disciple means turning toward and following he who manifests the kingly authority of God.

In Matthew, the call of the fisherman follows a sermon preached by Jesus. The theme of Jesus' sermon was "Repent, for the Kingdom of Heaven is at hand." Jesus was saying that the reign of God is here, time is up, and God is now active in human history. The Kingdom of Heaven is not in the future, but right now. One enters the Kingdom, which is at hand, by repenting and responding to the call of Jesus. In his book, *A Future for the Historical Jesus*, Leander Keck expresses well the relationship between repentance and discipleship:

When one undertakes to align his [sic] life with that of Jesus as model or paradigm, he restructures his life — that is, he repents. Immediately, it is apparent that Jesus revolutionizes repentance itself, for whereas John the Baptist required repentance as readiness for the coming of the Judge, Jesus summoned people to repent as a response to God's kingdom. Accordingly, in re-aligning the contours of one's life by trusting Jesus, one appropriates the central thrust of Jesus' own message: repentance as response. Since repentance is neither regret for not being religious sooner, nor remorse requisite for forgiveness, but the steady lifelong process of appropriating Jesus as one's paradigm, repentance holds together faith and ethics, religious trust and moral action. Repentance, so conceived, is not the prelude to Christian existence but the name of the game itself. To repent and to become a disciple (or to become a Christian) are the same thing — appropriating Jesus as trustworthy.

So, the kingdom is announced and people respond. The immediate response of the first four disciples is evidence of the "at-handness" of the Kingdom which Jesus proclaimed. No longer is it possible to sit on the sidelines and wait for some better offer to come along. The Kingdom, and the one who proclaimed it, demands a response.

William Willamon tells about going with his wife to the funeral of a friend, which was held in a little country church out in the backwoods. The minister took advantage of the occasion to berate those who had come: "You people need to decide for Jesus now. This dear, departed brother is safe because he had chosen Christ. Now is the time! Repent before it is too late!" After the service, Willamon said, "Can you get over that guy, taking advantage of having all of us there to beat us over the head about how it is important to make a decision right now."

"Yes," replied his wife, "and the worst thing about it is — he is right." (*Christian Century*, Fall 1986)

The Poor in Spirit

Most of us would say that the Beatitudes are well known and greatly loved by Christian people. They are beautiful. They dance and sing on the lips of those who say them. They have an unparalleled syntax that only the Jewish mind can capture and express. They are immortal. Hymns, anthems, songs, prayers, and liturgy have reflected upon their meaning and beauty.

Although we read them in our personal devotion because of their beauty, most of us do not get very excited about poverty of spirit, mourning, meekness, hunger and thirst for righteousness, mercifulness, purity of heart, peacemaking, and persecution for righteousness' sake. These are not the things that excite us. We become enthusiastic about qualities and values quite different from those expressed in the Beatitudes. We read the Beatitudes as people whose minds are shaped by an industrial, technological, marketplace mentality.

The word "blessed" in the Beatitudes literally means happy. But, the qualities expressed in the Beatitudes are not the common understanding of what it means to be happy. Happiness, for this generation, is a psychological state of inward satisfaction. The aim of happiness, as we understand it, is to feel good about ourselves and lives. Like the rising and setting of the sun, happiness seems to come and go in our lives. It is rarely constant. Although we chase after happiness for all we are worth, happiness, unlike blessedness, is dependent upon many external factors.

84

Blessedness, on the other hand, is deeper and far more inward than happiness. It is a state of being that is not primarily effected by the ebb and flow of life's tides. Unlike our ordinary view of happiness, has its roots in God. Blessedness comes because our life is dependent upon God. It is a gift from God which, according to the New Testament, comes to those who suffer because of their faithfulness. Blessedness is not a Hollywood kind of happiness. Instead, blessedness refers to a deep abiding happiness that can neither be given nor taken away by the world. It is well-being and prosperity: the gift of God to all people.

Today, I do not want to talk about all of the qualities expressed in the Beatitudes. I want to take one of them and see if it can shed light on the rest.

"Blessed are the poor in spirit for theirs is the Kingdom of Heaven." Notice that Jesus did not say, "Blessed are the poor." Jesus knew that blessedness was not tied to material poverty. The materially poor are not automatically happy, just as the materially wealthy are not automatically blessed. According to the Christian faith, happiness comes from the inside out and not from the outside in. It is not the kind of house that a person lives in, but the kind of person who lives in the house, that really matters. It's not the kind of clothing that a person wears, but the kind of person inside the clothing, that really counts. It's not the kind of church that a person goes to, but the kind of person inside the church, that has ultimate significance.

By saying, "Blessed are the poor in spirit," Jesus was driving at something very fundamental and quite basic. Jesus was saying, "Happy are those people who feel their spiritual poverty." If a person is poor, that person feels his or her poverty. Poverty is not academic or ethereal, but deeply felt inside of that human being. Therefore, Jesus meant "Blessed are those persons who feel their spiritual poverty. Blessed are those persons who are not certain of their own efficiency." In other words, Jesus was saying that we must first accept our spiritual poverty before we can begin a spiritual reformation.

Notice what Jesus did not say. Jesus did not say, "Blessed are those who have it all together." Jesus did not say, "Blessed are those who have all of the right answers." Jesus did not say, "Blessed are the people who have it all wrapped up, tied in bow, so that they understand it." Jesus did not say, "Blessed are the people who are certain of themselves." Jesus did not say, "Blessed are the people who have made sense out of everything." He did not say, "Blessed are the people who have their hands full of themselves." He did not say, "Blessed are the people who think they have it right on target every minute all of the time." He did not say, "Blessed are the know-it-alls."

Jesus said, "Blessed are those who know they don't have it all put together. Blessed are those who are not certain and yet keep questing. Blessed are those who are uncertain of themselves and yet seek certainty. Blessed are those who know that they have missed the mark and yet keep trying to find a better way." The acceptance of spiritual poverty is the prelude to blessedness.

In 1961, a group of students from the Vanderbilt Divinity School took a field trip to visit the Abbey of Our Lady of Gethsemane, a Trappist monastery located in central Kentucky. Thomas Merton, who was possibly the most famous Trappist monk of modern times, was still living at Gethsemane. Like the other monks who had chosen to live there, Thomas Merton had long since taken the Cistercian vows of celibacy, poverty, silence, and stability. He had given himself to a life of contemplation and prayer. Those seminarians who visited Gethsemane had the opportunity to visit with the now famous Thomas Merton. Little did most of them realize the greatness of the man who came and sat in their circle that day. His voice was soft and quiet. His eyes were deep and thoughtful. His character seemed to be in tune with the great harmony of God. Every square inch and every molecule of his body seemed to be filled with worship, quietness, prayer, and reflection. In the judgment of those seminarians, Thomas Merton was by every standard wealthy in the eyes of God. But, when Thomas

Merton described himself to those young seminary students, he depicted himself in a different way. With the quietness of an April morning he said, "I am spiritually poor." "Little do we realize," he continued, "the meaning of spiritual poverty, and the emptiness of desolation. The contemplation of God springs out of pure emptiness and genuine poverty." Although Thomas Merton had spent his life absorbing the life of Christ, he did not feel wealthy, but impoverished, in the eyes of God.

By contrast, most modern day Christians seem to have very little hunger for that which is spiritual. Our spiritual appetites have diminished. I am told by physicians that when one becomes sick, one of the symptoms of illness is the loss of appetite. Often when one becomes ill, one does not want to eat. Food turns the stomach. So it is with spiritual things. When we become spiritually sick, our spiritual appetite vanishes. Because we no longer have an appetite for that which is spiritual, many of us plod along trying to live vital lives with a tired and drab religion.

Or, perhaps, we have a misplaced hunger. Perhaps our need for security, power, and recognition is but another form of hunger for that which is eternal. When we are spiritually poor, we know that we cannot depend on ourselves. We know that we must depend on one who is greater. The poor in spirit are those who have a radical dependence on God that goes beyond dependence on the finite. The poor in spirit are those who have an earnest devouring hunger for God, while knowing that such hunger will never be satisfied and that the cup will never be full. The poor in spirit are those, who by their very nature, are thirsty and hungry for something outside of themselves.

Consider this possibility. Those who are hungry for God, those who have an appetite for the spiritual, those who are honestly seeking and questing — they are closer to God than some people who feel spiritually full and spiritually satisfied.

The poor in spirit are more like pilgrims than settlers. They are more like learners than like those who know it all. The poor in spirit are those who are open to new insights and new ways. They are those who know that their judgments are not absolute and final.

The great evangelist, E. Stanley Jones, once said, "We don't break God's laws, we break against them." Be certain of this fact: we do not break the Beatitudes, but if we live contrary to their spirit, we will break against them. If we try to live contrary to mercy, humility, goodness, purity, and all of the other qualities expressed, it is not the Beatitudes that will be shattered. It is those of us who live contrary to their spirit who will be broken.

The reasoning of this world begs us to live a style of life contrary to that of the Beatitudes. Our society teaches that blessedness comes by another route. The voices of our day say, "Blessed are those who are full. Blessed are those who are rich. Blessed are those who are successful. Blessed are those who are satisfied. Blessed are those who hold and wield power. Blessed are the beautiful people. Blessed are the upwardly mobile. Blessed are those who live on the sunny side of the street. Blessed are those who are not sick or frail, who do not make mistakes, and who never incurred the rejection of others because of a stand or position taken."

Those who are blessed are those who know the value of being spiritually poor. But, the problem is this: most of us are so full of everything that it rarely occurs to us to come empty before God.

A number of years ago, I became aware that I needed some dental work. I had a rather persistent toothache when I moved my tongue around the inside of my mouth, the spaces seemed like the Grand Canyon. Although I was aware that I needed dental help, I was very reluctant to go for help. I was not quite ready to accept it, much less, move on it.

I was with a rather modest parish at that time. In order to save some money, I decided that I would go to the University of Tennessee Dental School to let them look at my mouth and help me decide what kind of work I needed to have done.

They accepted me in a rather routine manner. They cleaned my teeth and took some x-rays of my mouth. The young hygienist who worked on me said, "Mr. Pennel, just stay here a little while." She brought in a student, and he got all excited. Then she brought in another student, and this student also got excited. Soon, I saw the students talking in another room. They had called the professor in and were discussing who would get to work on my mouth. A young dentist literally worked his way through Dental School on my mouth. He filled my teeth. He put in bridges. He capped and crowned. He worked on my gums. In fact, after he finished with me, he took an impression of my mouth. He was so proud of it. On the last day, he brought the impression with my name penciled in and said, "I'm going to keep this on my shelf for as long as I practice dentistry."

Until I accepted the poverty of my dental condition, I was not really ready to get my teeth fixed. I had to accept the poverty of my dental condition before I could be free to decide to get something done about it. So it is in our spiritual lives. Before our spiritual lives can grow, we first have to accept its poverty, its decay, and its need. Until we accept its decay and its poverty, we usually find no real motivation for its growth.

"Blessed are the poor in spirit for theirs is the Kingdom of Heaven."

Salt and Light

It's not easy to listen to Jesus tell us who we are and what we are to be in the world. At least one person listening to his sermon does not want to hear Jesus use a metaphor to describe and define what it is like to be one of his disciples.

We are tired of being defined and told what our purpose and function in life should be. Someone is always giving us a description of what our life should be like or look like.

As children, we were told to be little ladies and gentlemen. As adults, the culture in which we live tells us to work hard because only the fittest survive. It tells us get all we can because happiness consists of limitless material acquisition. Consume because consumption is inherently good. Become rich because property, power, and wealth are more important than people. Be progressive because progress is nothing but good.

And now, believe it or not, we have Jesus' words adding one more description and definition to our list of what and who we ought to be. His words only add to the long list of expectations already carefully recorded in our memory banks. These expectations come from our childhood, our youth, our culture, and now Jesus. "My followers," said Jesus, "are to be like salt and light."

Now that should be clear enough. Everyone knows what the purpose and function of salt and light are. The everyday purpose of salt is to preserve, flavor, and purify. Jesus was saying that his followers should preserve his teachings, flavor with love the lives of others, and purify that which has gone sour. That's who the followers of Jesus are. They are people who have a salt-like quality which adds to the lives of others. They function in a way that enhances or enriches the flavor of life.

The purpose of the disciple is defined by what he or she does. Just like the purpose of salt is defined by what it does. But, Jesus said there is a danger. We, as disciples, might become like salt which has lost its savor. Salt can lose its taste, and when it does, it is good for nothing except to be thrown out the window and trodden under the feet of those who pass by.

Likewise, a follower of Jesus can lose his or her salt-like quality and be good for nothing as a disciple of Jesus Christ. Saying that salt has lost its taste is like saying, "Bob was once a disciple;" or "Mary was once a follower;" "Bob once gave flavor to life, but for some reason, he quit doing it." So, add that one to your list of all that you are expected to be. You are to be the salt of the earth.

But Jesus also said that you are the light of the world. Everyone knows the purpose of light. Light casts out the darkness, enables others to see, and makes things visible. The worst thing that we can do with light is to hide it. If hidden, a light cannot push back the shadows, nor can it enable others to see.

There is a reason that we do not want to put the light of Christ on a stand so that all can see. We do not want to because we know that light draws unto itself.

The congregation I serve has been engaged in discussion about whether or not to house a Nashville Cares Office in our building. Nashville Cares is an organization devoted to supporting people with AIDS, understanding AIDS, and doing all that can be done to help persons who have contracted that dreaded disease. There are some people in our congregation who want to put the light of Christ on a stand so that people involved in that office and people with AIDS will be drawn to this church. But, there are other people in the church who want to put a bushel over the light because they do not want people with AIDS to be drawn to the light of Christ in this church. If we put the light of Christ on a stand, all kinds of people will be drawn to the church — alcoholics, drug addicts, juvenile delinquents, street people, yuppies, and people who are different.

It's easy to say that one should be like salt and light in a general sense. No one minds adding that to the list of what one should be and what one should do. But, how do we as individuals really live if we understand ourselves to be salt and light, not in a general sense, but in the everyday life?

What does it mean to be the salt of the earth and the light of the world when we are trying to decide between public education or private education for our children? What does it mean to be the salt of the earth and the light of the world when we are trying to decide how much to give away or how much to keep; how to get more and more material things so that we can be happier; how to negotiate time for our teenagers; how to get ready for a big dinner party, clean the house, and get the children where they need to be? What does it mean to be the salt of the earth and the light of the world when we are in the presence of a person who tells an ethnic joke? Do we laugh, turn aside, or say nothing? Often the telling of an ethnic joke says more about the person who tells it than it does about the person who hears it.

I have a friend who is a chaplain at the Middle Tennessee Mental Health Institute. In 1987 he wrote the following annual report concerning his ministry. I have a feeling that my friend has discovered what it means to be salt and light.

My calling is to a mental health institute. My ministry is among folks who have special needs, distorted judgments, and peculiar perceptions about themselves and their environment. All these things make my work a little unique. Yet in other ways, it is very much like any other parish.

I WORSHIP WITH MY PEOPLE. We have regular Sunday worship services with a volunteer organist, bulletins, good and not-so-good preaching, and a monthly observance of Holy Communion. There are four chaplains on the staff, so my rotation is about once a month.

During the worship service, many usual and unusual things may happen. People will sing the hymns, especially if they are familiar ones, join in the responsive and unison readings, and sit quietly during the sermon. Then again, others may yell out a certain hymn they would like to sing, ask to sing a solo, come forward to kneel during most any part of the service for a moment of prayer, or come forward and stand beside me while I am preaching. I have had more than a few walk out at what I considered to be a crucial point in the sermon — a humbling reminder that it is God's Word, and not mine, that is being proclaimed.

Beyond these expected surprises, however, is the reverence and attention that is part of their participation in the service. We have people, of course, who at the end of the service will express the customary appreciation of the service and the sermon. But more than that is what can be seen in the eyes of the worshipers, that acknowledgement and recognition that lets you know that, by the Grace of God, simple words are connecting with a deeper part of their "wholeness" and "health".

I NURTURE MY PEOPLE. One of the new ways in which this nurturing is happening is through a group I started along with a music therapist, Helen Baker, who also plays the organ at the Hillcrest United Methodist Church in Nashville.

The group consists largely of the more regressed people. That is, these folks are more impaired because of their delusions and hallucinations, less oriented to time and place, more confused and less able to interact socially. Helen and I have created a group that combines music (music somehow reaches a very primitive core of their experience) and a caring community. We have selected a number of religious songs — some gospel, some spiritual (which we sing to movement), and some religious folk. Intermittent with the singing, we have discussions about a holiday coming up, an affirmation of a group member, a Bible narrative, or a particular Thanksgiving.

Group members do not just come to group meetings. They belong to the group. And, because they belong, they have an opportunity to share their individual gifts. Group members may lead their favorite songs, pass out the songbooks, arrange the chairs, help serve the coffee, and do assignments which may mean research in the library. We assume that everyone has a gift and grace to offer, if provided an opportunity.

The important aspect of this is how we are instruments for the coaxing out to take place. Helen and I both are taught daily in this process by these folks. We learn and re-learn, forget and re-learn again what special powers are hidden away in these people. I think about Clarence, who when asked to lead a hymn, stood, paused, took a minute to tuck in his shirt and lead the hymn. Thank you, Lord, for Clarence. But that is another story.

I CREATE OPPORTUNITIES FOR MY PEOPLE TO NURTURE. Several years ago I had a group called "Care-Givers." In the group, four or five people would visit, on a weekly basis, one elderly lady in the geriatrics program. Working from this earlier model, I have begun this year to create a variety of situations in which people can offer care to others. On an advanced level, some people do things individually. One lady plays the piano for an assembly program in the geriatrics building twice a week. One man visits another man twice a week and provides a leisure activity for him. Another man visits one of the more regressed men, helps him purchase food from the commissary, takes him for walks, and helps him write letters to his grandmother.

On a more basic level, some people meet in a group to plan a social event for other "less fortunate" people in the

Institute. The group chooses the people, plans the activity, sends out the invitations, prepares the refreshments, and hosts the event. We have held three such events since the first of September. The last and biggest was the Christmas party for thirty-five men in the mentally retarded secure facility. My people baked cookies, made gifts, ordered food from the dietary, sang Christmas songs, and hosted the event.

I INVOLVE MY RELIGIOUS COMMUNITY WITH MY PEOPLE. I cannot say how grateful I am to the youth and adults of Belmont United Methodist Church. Their generosity has been overwhelming. In the late winter, they helped a lady who was discharged set up her apartment. The church members provided some much needed furniture. The youth helped her paint her apartment. A church family loaned her a bike for transportation. On several Sundays a family gave her a ride to and from church.

In June, the youth came to the Institute to present their musical. We had hoped thirty patients would attend. Seventy showed up. Amazingly, the people were attentive and responsive. Only a few walked out. Later, many said how much the program had meant to them. The most worshipful moment for me was when Gloria, who is autistic and withdrawn, stood for one of the numbers. She had been so moved that she had to dance and clap, which she did.

In October, the youth group sponsored a picnic. As always, there was an abundance of food. Likewise, there was a lot of interaction at the table for checkers, chess, and cards, and also during the baseball game. One person expressed his appreciation for the opportunity to go and stated that what had impressed him the most was the group's acceptance of Emma, who had stood during the singing and had insisted on singing a solo.

In December, the youth sponsored a trip to Opryland. This was the second year. We met at the church, paired off, rode an MTA bus, enjoyed a leisurely evening, and came back to the church for refreshments and gifts. Marvelous and mysterious.

Belmont United Methodist Church is not the only church that comes to the Institute to provide programs of nurture and support. There is a long list of other volunteers. What makes Belmont's care unique and special is that it is the only church that takes the people off grounds for the activities. I believe that is fundamental to the quality of their care and compassion. To the extent that Belmont does that, it relates in a more trusting and accepting way. And, it relates to the patients more as people and less as simply patients.

It is not only important to think about how individuals understand themselves to be salt and light, but we must also reflect on how the church lives when it understands itself as salt and light. Does the church spend more of its resources on buildings or people? On the national church or local mission? Music or Christian education? On pastoral care or prophetic witness? On individuals or on larger groups of people?

To say that we are the salt of the earth and the light of the world is to understand ourselves in a certain way.

Let us not forget that when we understand ourselves as salt and light, we need to be very careful about who gets the credit. Jesus said that it is okay for people to see your good works; but, people should also give glory to your Father who is in heaven because of what they see. The church goes about its work in the world not to call attention to itself, but to point beyond itself to the one in whose name it ministers and works.

My friend, Ray, and many patron saints of the rank and file go about their work as Christ's people not in a self-congratulatory way, but in a way which gives God the glory.

Settling
Our Differences

On the surface "Tribute" is a motion picture about a man
who is diagnosed with cancer and about his response to that
disease. But at a much deeper level, "Tribute" is about a man
who is not reconciled to his own son. "Tribute" is about a
father and son who needed to settle their differences. Like those
characters in "Tribute," one of the persistent needs of our
life is to settle our differences.

There are many ways that we try to settle our differences.
Some of us try to settle our differences by taking flight. In
so doing, we try to settle our differences by flying away from
them. We try to handle our differences by not handling them.
We try to settle our differences by ignoring them. We try to
settle our differences by putting our heads in the sand like the
proverbial ostrich. At other times we try to settle our differences by taking flight with excessive drugs, alcohol, and bar-
bituates. Taking flight is one of the ways that many of us
handle our differences.

Others of us try to handle our differences not by taking
flight, but by fighting back. We clench our fists and set our
jaws. We practice an eye-for-an-eye-and-a-tooth-for-a-tooth
kind of ethics. We harbor a grudge. We act out our resent-
ments, and we believe that every punishment should be equal
to every offense.

Still others of us try to settle our differences by traveling the path of compromise. We choose to live in the land of compromise, whose primary symbol is a very high tolerance level for those who differ with us. The spirit of compromise has its place, but, at times, compromise can keep us from dealing creatively with differences that exist between ourselves and others.

In almost every area of life, we need to learn how to handle our differences. We need to learn to handle the differences between ourselves and the significant others in our lives — our mate, our child, our best friend, or a colleague with whom we work. Psychologists often list symptoms of a spiritual divorce. These symptoms are most often applied to marriage, but they can also be applied to the break up of any significant relationship.

When people start breaking up with each other, some symptoms begin to appear. First, separating people, become quietly indifferent to one another. Next, there is a coolness where persons treat one another with a cold shoulder or with a frozen stare. Next, there is lack of tenderness where touching, feeling, and talking in soft voices seems to be absent resulting in routine communication. After a while, there is only enough communication to keep things going. A little boy was asked, "What do you talk about at your house?"

He said, "We don't talk about anything except, at meals. We say 'pass the salt' and 'pass the pepper,' but that's about all."

Next, there's a feeling of not being understood. We feel like others do not understand us. And, if others would understand us, we could get along much better with each other. Feeling builds upon feeling, until there is tension which expresses itself with sarcasm and ridicule. Finally, there is no shared ethos, or spiritual life.

If we do not learn to settle our differences with those we love and who are closest to us, we can drift farther and farther apart until we become like ships passing in the night.

Often it is not the big things that separate us from each other. It is not the mountains that we climb. It is more often the sand in our shoes which causes us to be irritable toward one another. Little things like sulkiness, moodiness, irritability, petty jealousy, quarreling, nagging, and short fuses cause us to be separated from one another. These are the things that often make us unfit to live with.

Breakups, which occur within significant relationships between persons, do not come first. Rather, separating significant people from each other often comes last, after a long series of differences have quietly eroded the relationship.

Consider the possibility that we also need to learn to handle our differences in the larger social arena. The church that I serve sponsors an annual brotherhood-sisterhood banquet. This is an occasion for blacks, Jews, Roman Catholics, and Anglo-Saxon Protestants to come together for a meal, fellowship, and a program. A recent program dealt with the nature of prejudice and how prejudice works in our lives. As I sat through that program, I found myself reflecting on a very simple but basic thought. I found myself saying, "If we, as extremely diverse people, had learned over the years how to handle our differences, how much pain we would have avoided." But, because we have not learned to settle our differences in the social arena and on the international stage, we continue, and shall continue, to pay a higher and higher price. And, that price might someday be higher than any of us really wants to pay. The survival of humankind demands that we learn how to settle our differences at the national and international level.

The Scripture lesson for today speaks about two ways to handle our differences. The first is to learn to live by the ethics of a higher righteous. According to this higher ethic, it is not only wrong to murder, it is also morally wrong to hate. If I had the power to call a great world summit and could give the leaders of the world a topic to consider, I would not ask them to talk about how to stop war or how to deter "Star Wars."

I would not ask them how to stop the arms race. Rather I would ask, "What is it that causes us to be angry with each other?" I would beg the leaders of the world to probe that question, to study it, and to reflect upon it. If we could understand what it is that causes people to be angry with each other, then the symptom of anger, which is war, would go away. The symptom of anger, which is crime, would be diminished. The symptom of anger, which is revenge, would disappear.

In Jesus' day the law was very clear. It said that people should not murder each other. But, Jesus called people to a higher standard by saying, "It is not only wrong to murder, it is also morally wrong to hate one another." In the teaching of Jesus, the inward disposition becomes more important than the overt act. The motive became more important than the deed. Who we are becomes more important than what we do. That is the higher ethic. That's the greater standard. That is the better righteousness. The law, though important and necessary, can only take us so far. We need, for example, to enact laws in this country which will guarantee women equal opportunity in every phase of life. But, that's the very least we can do. Passing laws which will guarantee my daughters the same opportunity that I had is crucially important, but such laws, written in books and enacted by legislators, will not take us far enough. We can pass all of the legislation we wish; but, if our hearts do not change, we will find ways to deny women opportunities which correspond with their interests and their abilities.

Jesus did not say, "Let your righteousness be based upon a whim morality." Nor did he say, "Let your righteousness be based upon what your reference group thinks." Nor did he utter, "Let your righteousness be based upon what everybody else does." In justifying a position my daughters will often say, "Everybody else is doing it." But, Jesus did not say, "Let your righteousness be based upon what everybody else does." Nor did he say, "Let your righteousness be based upon what self-centeredness declares to be right." But, he did call us to let our righteousness exceed that of conventional morality. Let it go further than the herd mind. Let it be rooted in a different standard.

To live by a higher ethic that does not permit anger nor insult is the prelude to settling our differences. The conventional law said, "Thou shall not kill." That's all that was required. But, Jesus taught that everyone who is angry is liable for judgement. It's not enough not to kill. To be angry with someone else makes us liable for the judgment of God.

Matthew wants us to learn a fundamental and basic lesson. Matthew wants us to learn that if we are hung up with each other we are also hung up with God. To be hung up with another human being is also to be at odds with God. In that teaching, Jesus lifted the differences between us to a divine dimension.

Today's Scripture lesson indicates a second way for us to settle our differences. Said Matthew, "So if you are offering your gift at the altar, and there remember that your brother has something against you, leave your gift there before the altar and go; first be reconciled to your brother and then come and offer your gift." According to this, being reconciled to one another is far more important than whatever gift one might leave at the altar. In fact, if we are not reconciled to each other, the gift that we leave at the altar is robbed of its meaning. There is no way to mistake the truth. If we want to be at one with God, we need to be at one with each other. There is no way for us to be at one with God and not strive to be at one with each other. To be at odds with another person is also to be at odds with God.

Settling the differences that exist between people is crucial. And, such differences can be settled if we live by the higher righteousness and seek to be reconciled to each other. If we do not live by a higher standard and seek reconciliation, our differences will not go away. Instead, they will fester and grow until we are separated more and more from others, from ourselves, and, ultimately, from God.

Jesus put this whole issue another way when he said, "Whatsoever you would do that people do unto you, do you even so unto them." In other words, "Love your neighbor as yourself."

The Primacy of Human Relationships

People being properly related to one another was important to Jesus. He spoke with great clarity about the primacy of human relationships. He wanted good relationships to be maintained. The re-establishment of broken relationships was a central concern. According to his teaching a person who was not properly related to others could not be properly related to God. People loving God by loving each other was of ultimate significance.

We are living in a society which does not stress the primary importance of human relationships. Other things are more important than the ultimate significance of people being properly joined to one another.

For many people "the bottom line" is more crucial. "What is the bottom line?" is commonly asked about almost every concern. For college students, the bottom line is the grade posted at the termination of the semester. For business people, the bottom line is the final figure in the profit and loss column. For athletic teams, the bottom line is the number posted on the scoreboard when the final second of the game ticks away. For church officials, the bottom line is how much money has been raised and how many members have been received.

In Pat Conroy's book, *The Prince of Tides*, there is a

character who yearns to have one of her recipes printed in the most prominent cookbook in the city of Colleton, South Carolina. She does everything in her power to get her pet recipe in Colleton's premiere cookbook. She experiments with various food combinations. She presents herself to those people who will make the decision about which recipes will and will not be accepted. For her, getting a recipe in the fashionable cookbook was the bottom line. Her validity as a worthwhile person depended on seeing her name in that book.

When I was in high school, I worked in my uncle's plumbing shop. Every plumber and helper in that plumbing company did greasy, filthy work except for Raymond Brigance. Raymond did what we called "inside work." He went from house to house repairing sink faucets and fixing toilet tanks. His work did not require many tools and not many parts. Raymond was never called upon to dig a ditch, clean a sewer, repair water lines, install a hot water tank, or put in drain lines. His work was ordered, predictable, and clean. Every single plumber at Hill Services wanted Raymond's job. Getting Raymond's job was the bottom line for those plumbers whose work was forever in the sludge. Raymond's job was, for them, the symbol of success and the top of the ladder.

Today's Gospel lesson speaks about the bottom line in the teachings of Jesus. The bottom line, for Jesus, was the "tending to" and the maintenance of strong relationships among people. His teaching about swearing clearly illustrates the primacy of personal relationships. Jesus said that his followers should not swear falsely. Nor should they swear at all. They should not swear by something as high as heaven, as common-place as the earth, or as spectacular as the city of Jerusalem. Swearing will not change things. It will not change our physical characteristics like the color of our hair. "Let what you say be simply 'Yes' or 'No'; anything more than this comes from evil," taught Jesus.

Disciples of Jesus should have an integrity of character that does not need the scaffolding of an oath to persuade others of her or his truthfulness. Disciples do not need super-structure to support their words. Truth, for the disciple, does not need to call in outside help. The disciple who tries to live by the standards of "over-abundant" righteousness does not need any props for truth-telling. This was "bottom line" talk for Jesus. And, there was a reason that Jesus spoke about the importance of integrity. It is almost impossible to be related to one another when truth is absent. Sound human relationships can only be built on the foundation of truthfulness. Not telling the truth destroys human relationships. It is difficult to have a good relationship with a person who is perceived as not telling the truth. Likewise, it is difficult for others to live with us if we are perceived as not "ringing true."

Truthfulness, as a bottom-line way of life, is facing hard times today. The keynote speaker at the National Democratic Convention said, "they [the Republicans] have lied to us." The Republican response said that the Democrats were dishonest in their presentation of the way things are. Both parties had assumed that the other political faction had lied. Political parties cannot live in correct relationship to each other if it is passively assumed that each lies to the other. Countries cannot be properly related to each other if both assume that the other is lying. Dubbing Russia an "Evil Empire" does not foster truth among nations. Labeling the U.S.A. an "Imperialist Aggressor" does not add a plank to the foundation of truth.

This notion about truth being the glue for national and international relationships also holds true in the area of personal relationships. In my almost thirty years as a pastor, I have officiated at hundreds of funerals. Most, though not all, of these funerals have called for a homily, a time to proclaim the Christian faith in the face of death. In many of these homilies, I have spoken about the values to which the life of the deceased had witnessed. In some of these services of death and resurrection, I have not been able to say that the person, while living, practiced a life of integrity. When I have not been able to say that one thing, one of the most important things that could be said has gone unsaid. No higher compliment can come to a person than to say that he or she spoke and lived the truth as he or she understood it.

Which is more important: to say that a person earned and spent a fortune, or to say that a person needed no scaffolding for truth-telling? To say that a person climbed to the top of his or her profession or to say that integrity was practiced? To say that a person hit a home run every time he or she got up to bat, or to say that he or she was a person who knew how to say "yes" and "no"?

Surely, there is at least one person here today who knows the importance of being honest, but who has a difficult time being a truthful person in the "everydayness" of life. All of us know how difficult it is to quietly and humbly tell the truth. Deciding to risk telling the truth is one thing; living that out in the concreteness of daily life is another. How often simple truthfulness breaks against the rock of everyday mundane existence! The slow, endless, lapping of the waves does more to turn rocks to sand than the fury of the occasional storm. Not speaking and living the truth, in things both large and small, can grind us up into people who cannot be trusted and on whom others cannot depend.

But, it is not easy to humbly follow the admonition of Jesus to say "yes" and "no". It is not easy because we believe that not being truthful will gain us some advantage in life. It is not easy because speaking the truth will, in some situations, bring opposition and rejection. It is not easy because truth is often slippery, error is subtle, and there is a human appetite for illusion. It is not easy because we have to decide with less than perfect knowledge. But, nothing should be of higher value to the Christian than to see the triumph of truth. We should pray passionately that it will prevail. And, we are called by Jesus to love it more than our own prestige or sense of security. Christianity teaches that to love the truth and to love God are one and the same. It is so crucial that none of us wants to see truth overcome by our hands. Without it, relationships are broken;

and we, as individuals, are compromised. But it was a bottom line for Jesus, and so it should be for those of us who follow after his way.

In May of 1988, sixteen-year-old Matt Turner was unceremoniously yanked out of the Tennessee state high school tennis tournament by his dad. That put-a-foot down stand by a parent was so stunning that it drew national attention. The story appeared in *USA Today* and was related on radio by Paul Harvey. A woman from Des Moines, Iowa, contacted a Tennessee newspaper seeking to congratulate the boy's father.

Hence, he was cast in the eyes of the nation as "Matt the Brat," symbol of the quintessential kiddie tennis menace. After Matt had cooled down, he had just one thing to say to his father for creating all of the embarrassing notoriety: "Thanks."

"I didn't talk to him for a day after the incident," says Matt, who has continued to play the school-boy circuit. "We did not ride home together after he pulled me out of the state tournament. He left right away, and I stayed and rode home with my coach. But, the next night at home, my dad called me in and we sat down together and talked about what had happened, why he did what he did. He explained that he did it for my own good. He said that he did not want to see me acting that way in public, that I was hurting myself even if I did not see it at the time.

"He said he knew that he made me mad, embarrassed me, and hurt my feelings, but he hoped that I understood that he did what he felt was in my best interest."

Did he buy that?

"Yes, I did," said Matt. "I have all of the respect in the world for my father. I believed every word he told me. I know he did what he did because he cares about me, and I appreciate it."

Matt, a polite youngster off the court with a tendency to grow horns when play starts, says he's better for the experience. But, he admits that he was angry and confused at the time.

"It was kinda hard to take," he said. "I couldn't believe my father had made me forfeit the match like that." In the TSSAA Tournament, Turner wasn't playing well and the crowd was razzing him. "They were really on my case," he recalls. "I finally let everything get to me — playing badly and the crowd and everything. I guess I kinda lost my temper." Matt made obscene gestures at his tormentors. The crowd got even rougher. Matt responded with more gestures. And, suddenly, his father was at courtside, instructing the coach to get his son off the court.

"I've seen enough," said Larry Turner, a Knoxville restaurant comptroller. "Go tell him to put up his racquet."

During a July 1988, tournament at Duke University an opponent wandered over and asked Matt if he was "the" Matt Turner — the one he had read about in *USA Today*.

"I told him I was," said Matt, adding, "That was a tough way to become famous." It was tough — tough because Matt happened to have a father who acted upon what he considered to be his bottom line.

I do not know if Matt's father goes to church, reads his Bible, or prays on a daily basis. Perhaps he is religious. Perhaps he is not. Religious or not, he did not need to call in outside help in speaking to his son. He did not resort to swearing. He just said "no" to the behavior of his son. As a result of his honesty, there is now, and probably always will be, a strong relationship between that father and his son. What if Matt's father had not acted? What if he had been silent? What if his bottom line had been "win at any price"? What if winning the trophy had been more important than playing the game with decorum?

I expect there were some church-going, Bible-reading, praying people in the stands that day who would not have done what Matt's father did. Who is closer to God? Those who are consistent in their religious practice, but who would say nothing. Or, those who never darken the church door, but whose words are simply "yes" and "no".

If you had been sitting in the stands that day, would a solid relationship with your son, based upon integrity, be more important than a victory trophy?

"Let what you say be simply 'yes' or 'no'." Those who care about the primacy of relationships will not need the scaffolding of an oath to persuade others about that which is true.

Beyond the Ordinary

At 7:00 a.m. every Monday, I teach Bible study. About twenty of us meet from 7:00-7:15 a.m. for coffee, juice, and a light breakfast. Each week, a different member of the group brings the food for the rest of the crowd. The fare consists of biscuits, muffins, bagels, and various breads complete with the appropriate condiments. For fifteen minutes, we sip hot coffee and nibble on high-calorie homemade delights. After breaking our fast, we settle in for the Monday morning Bible study.

When we studied Matthew 5:38-48, one member of our group said, "What Jesus said sounds good, but it will not work in real life." Well, I want us to see if we can hear what Jesus is saying. I want us to see if his words can speak to our situation today. Will the truth of Jesus' words hold up in the real world? Will the truth of Jesus' words work in a world which sees truth in a very different way?

The world's truth nods with great assurance and says, "An eye for an eye and a tooth for a tooth." But, Jesus' truth takes a differant position. It says that disciples should "resist not evil." The violence of the wrongdoer should not be met by violence, either by way of revenge or by getting one's blow in first. This requires a radical change in the attitudes of disciples. The attitude required by Jesus is only possible if we learn to despise suffering. If we despise the suffering that can be inflicted on us, then we must also despise the suffering that we have the capability of inflicting on others. Thus, we, as disciples of Christ, should resist evil and overcome it with good.

Overcoming evil with good is more than mere non-resistance. It is responding to active enmity with active love. Jesus used three extreme examples to illustrate his point. Those who live by the higher ethic of over-abundant righteousness are to turn the other cheek, give away undergarments, go the second mile, and give to any who borrow. In my judgment, these are not laws to be obeyed. Here, a certain spirit is being commended. These regulations are not to be slavishly carried out. But, this does not give us license to evade the demand which Jesus put forth in the extreme case. Jesus meant what he said; his followers are to manifest the spirit of His teaching in the various situations that arise in real life.

It is not difficult to see that the truth of Jesus and the truth of the world are not the same. Jesus' truth stands for overcoming evil with good. The world's truth screams at us to meet violence with violence.

But we must admit that the truth of Jesus is not very practical in a world like this. When Jesus said what he said, did he know what our world would be like? Ours is a society in which violence and crime are increasing at an alarming rate. Illegal drugs have become the curse of the century — a plague as virulent and as deadly to our cities as the plagues of the Middle Ages were — wrecking a kind of societal havoc against which we seem to be defenseless. They tell us that there are all sorts of people on drugs, and that these people are trying to get more and more money so they can buy more and more drugs. They tell us that if we leave our cars unlocked in Hillsboro Village, in Brentwood, or in Belle Meade, we are doing so at our own peril.

What are United Methodists to do about situations like this? How are we to respond? First, we should do what everybody else does about it because we are very much like the rest of the world. We should lock our doors and take precautions. There is nothing un-Christian about protecting ourselves and those we love from harm. If that is all that we are expected to do — to protect ourselves — we could close this service right now and go home early. But, that is not all. We, as Christians, are also not to spend our time and energy trying to figure out how to get even with those who are involved in drug traffic. That would be the easy thing to do. There is another part — the hard part. Christians should respond entirely different from the way the rest of the world responds. The hard part, according to Matthew, is not responding to evil with evil. The hard part is trying to discern what it means to go the second mile with those who would do us harm. The hard part is attempting to live the truth of Jesus in a world that does not know and does not care about the truth of Jesus. At times, it is difficult to know which is the genuine truth — the Gospel's truth or the world's truth. Most of the time, we live in the land somewhere between the truth of the Gospel and the truth of the world. Often, we are not willing to trust the ways of the Gospel's truth. But once we have met the Gospel's truth, something makes us very uneasy with the path of the world's truth.

It is difficult to live out the Gospel's truth because what controls Christians also happens to control non-Christians — very human instincts and impulses. And yet, Jesus said that there is another possibility. There is the possibility that when we are controlled by what love demands, we will be different from other people. When we are controlled by the spirit that lies behind turning the other cheek and going the second mile, we are not like the rest of the world. The society in which we live measures itself by the standard of an "eye for an eye and a tooth for a tooth." The difference between these two ways of relating to others is vast and almost incomprehensible.

Christians also live by a different truth when they practice love toward their enemies. The world's truth calls people to love their neighbors and to hate their enemies. Jesus held up the notion that we should love our enemies and pray for those who persecute us.

"Thou shalt love thy neighbor." (Leviticus 19:18) It is

crystal clear that, by "neighbor," Leviticus meant fellow —
Israelite. The Rabbis gave to "neighbor" the widest possible
meaning by including under the term not only born Israelites,
but also converts to Judaism from the Gentile nations. There
was nothing in Leviticus 19:18 to indicate to a Jew, in Jesus'
day, that he ought to love Pontius Pilate. Indeed, there was
a great deal in the first five books of the Old Testament to
justify the opposite. Since the Pentateuch was regarded as in-
spired, it was clearly understood that love was limited to certain human boundaries. It is not surprising that devoted Jews
inferred from Leviticus 19:18 that their duty was to love their
fellow-Jews and to dislike their Roman enemies. But, Jewish
literature does not yield any evidence that such a conclusion
can be explicitly drawn. In my research, "Thou shalt love thy
neighbor and hate thine enemy" cannot be found. This infers
that the words "and hate thine enemy" are an interpolation.
With the antithesis removed, the true force of the saying pushes
into the light. The true meaning of this saying is simply "Love
your enemies as well as your friends," and not "Love your
enemies rather than hate them."

This love for enemies and friends is shown in three con-
crete examples. First is the appeal to God's way. In the order
of nature, God grants sunshine and rain to both friend and
foe. God loves both so much that the common watering of
the earth is held from neither.

Secondly, the "higher righteousness" required of disciples
demands much more than the sort of kindness and affection
found among publicans and Gentiles, to say nothing of that
found among Scribes and Pharisees. This conventional kindness is no longer sufficient for disciples of Jesus.

Thirdly, the higher standard that followers of Jesus strive
for is the perfection that can be found in God. Since God's
love is displayed for all persons, disciples should embody that
same love.

Perhaps, the lady at Bible study is correct. Maybe this
teaching of Jesus does not work out in real life. Perhaps, the

truth of this passage does run counter to society's view of truth. Jesus never thought about the practicality of this passage. Obviously, it was not very practical for Jesus. He wound up on a cross because he practiced it. It certainly did not "work" in his life. Instead, it contributed to his Crucifixion, the death penalty for an insurrectionist.

What then is Matthew saying to us? The Sermon on the Mount, we now believe, was written by Matthew to give to new converts — people who had just been baptized. When people had been baptized and received into the church, the Sermon on the Mount was the document that Matthew helped put together to give to these new believers. Matthew was saying that a certain kind of love makes the church distinctive. Matthew, no doubt, used extremes in order to make his point. Christians cannot love themselves and others in the characteristic way. Instead, there is, for Christians, a distinctive characteristic. Matthew was saying that Christians are to love in ways that go beyond the ordinary — to turn the other cheek, to go the extra mile, to give away their underwear, and to have sympathy for those who beg and borrow. That is the kind of love that distinguishes the Christian love from conventional, ordinary love.

But Matthew was also saying that Christians are called upon to love beyond the boundaries of life. "If you love only those who love you, what reward have you?" he said. He was saying that, as Christians, we should try to practice a distinct kind of love that cuts across barriers and jumps over boundaries. Blacks can love whites, and whites can love blacks. People under thirty can love those over thirty, and people over thirty can love those under thirty. Blue-collar workers can love those in management, and those in management can love blue-collar people. Activists can love conservatives, and conservatives can love activists. Those in establishment can love hippies, and hippies can love those in establishment. The militant can love the pacifist, and the pacifist can love the militant.

Why do you think Matthew asked his readers to practice

the kind of love that has no boundaries? I have a feeling that
Jesus asked us to love beyond boundaries because Jesus knew
that through loving our enemies, we would wind up loving ourselves. We become more and more loving as we learn to love
those who oppose us. We become more and more loving as
we learn to love those who differ from us. We become more
and more loving as we try to love those who hurt us and strike
back at us.

As I learn to love my enemy, I find that I have a healthier
self-love. Jesus loved sinners and lepers and tax collectors, not
only to save sinners and lepers and tax collectors, but also to
save the Pharisees. Paul loved the Gentiles, not only to save
the Gentiles, but also to save Israel. We are called upon to
love our enemies that we might be saved.

I grew up in a neighborhood that had a nickname. The nickname for my neighborhood was "Pinch". I suppose that my
neighborhood got that nickname because those of us who lived
there were always in a pinch. Economically and socially, we
were always in a pinch. As I grew up in "Pinch," I was
programmed by my community, my family, and my church
to know my enemies. As a child, I knew who my enemies were.
"Pinch" had taught me that. The institutions had taught it;
the family had taught it; the social environment had taught
it. I can still rattle the labels back to you. I am not proud of
that, but that's the way it was. My enemies in the early For-
ties were Japs, Jews, Catholics, Blacks, and the little Chinese
families who ran the stores in our neighborhood. I knew who
they were. I had been programmed to believe that they were
the outsiders, and I was an insider. They were my enemies,
and I had to do something to resist them and to stand against
them.

In "Pinch," I knew where the boundaries were. I knew
that there was an invisible line that separated "Pinch" from
Railroad Shanty Town. And, another invisible line separated
"Pinch" from the Hollywood community. Another invisible
line separated "Pinch" from Chickasaw Gardens, the home

of the wealthy. I knew where I belonged. I belonged within my boundaries. That was clearly understood.

Now, I want to be very honest in saying that learning to get rid of those boundaries and learning to love those enemies has been a painful journey for me. And, I am not there yet. There are still reservoirs of hatred in my life that continue to fester like a cesspool. But as I have gone along, I have learned that the more I love my enemies, the better I feel about myself. The more I have learned to cross boundaries, the more loving I have become. At one period in my life, I set out to love my enemy so that my enemy would become better. Now, I know that's not the case. Whenever I have loved my enemy, I have become more loving.

The lesson for today is that we are to love, not only our neighbors but our enemies as well. But how do we find the strength to live out Jesus' truth when it is contrary to the world's truth? Matthew said that we find the strength by praying for those who persecute us. When we pray earnestly, persistently, and lovingly for those who oppose us, something unexpected often happens. That "unexpected something" is that we begin to change. We begin to see life differently. We begin to understand why a particular people and a certain group are wired up the way they are. Through prayer we find the needed resource to love, not only our enemies, but also our friends. It takes constant prayer to overcome evil with good. It requires not one minute of prayer to meet violence with violence, to not go the second mile, to not turn the other cheek, to not give to those who ask, and to turn away from those who want to borrow. Praying for those who stand against us is the only way to find the kind of love that reaches out to both friends and enemies. And, we must not deter from this because Jesus put it on the line when he said, "If you love only those who love you, what reward have you?"

This way of living and looking at life is beyond the ordinary.

Fog-Clearing Moments

Remember that fog we had last November? I had to venture into it early that Sunday morning. I left home about 6:00 a.m., long before most people even thought about getting up. The fog was dense. My automobile headlights would not cut it. Visibility was reduced to about ten feet. I turned on my dimmer lights and hoped that on-coming traffic would do the same. As I drove, I felt like my car was pushing through a tunnel of smoke.

I was able to drive from my house to the church because I had driven along that route so many times. I knew the hills, curves, landmarks, and the names of intersecting streets. I knew when I was passing the college, the elementary school, the international restaurant, and the grocery store. I knew when I was passing those places, not because I could see them, but because the roadway told me where I was. I knew the road well because I had driven it so many crystal clear days. I had to trust in my memories of a time when there was not any fog in order to get myself through the fog.

A great portion of life is like living in fog. We are not certain of what is around us, where we are going, what or who might be around the next curve. We creep along the roads of life without a clear vision of what has happened, what is happening, or what will happen next. Trying to find our way through social problems, political problems, economic difficulties, family troubles, and personal anxieties is more like threading through fog than flying down an open road. Often we have to follow the road even when we are most uncertain of where it leads.

Likewise, matters of faith and belief are more like a fog than a clear day. Most of us live in a fog when it comes to questions like, "Who is God?", "What is God like?", and "How does God interact within human life?" What we believe and how we came to believe it are not clear to us. Theology is more ambiguous than it is plain. Figuring out what we believe and why, is often accomplished without clear understanding.

Even the first disciples lived in a fog about the identity of Jesus. Though they had decided to follow him, they were unclear about his identity or purpose. The Gospel writers are careful to point out that the disciples did not understand the purpose of Jesus' ministry. "Who is Jesus?" seems to dominate the thinking of the New Testament. Some saw him as the royal Davidic Messiah. Others saw him as the earthly Son of Man who called his followers into suffering discipleship. He was to some the new Moses. Others saw him as being like Moses and Elijah, yet even greater. For others, he was the Anointed Servant of God, the Beloved Son who shares in the glory of God. Because the disciples did not understand, they were often filled with awe, amazement, and fear. Even after the Transfiguration, the disciples did not fully understand who Jesus was or where his mission would take him. As they descended the mountain after the Transfiguration, Jesus charged them with secrecy "until the Son of Man is raised from the dead." But the disciples were totally in the dark about Jesus. They had him confused with Elijah and John the Baptizer.

But, the fact remains that those first disciples persisted in following Jesus, even when they could not see clearly. They followed him even when they did not understand. They stayed on the road with him, even when the fog was so thick that it could have been cut with a knife. That is, they stayed with him until the cross loomed large and heavy. Then they deserted. But, until then, they followed though the way was not clear.

Perhaps the story of the Transfiguration gives us a clue to understanding the disciples' ability to follow, even when they did not understand. Jesus took four of the disciples with him to a high mountain. While there, he was transfigured before them. His face became as bright as the sun. His garments became as white as light. Moses and Elijah appeared and had a conversation with Jesus. Peter got all excited and offered to build three booths, one for Jesus, one for Moses, and one for Elijah. While Peter was speaking, a voice came from a cloud and said, "This is my beloved Son, with whom I am well pleased. Listen to him." The disciples were so moved by this identification of Jesus that they fell on their faces and were filled with awe.

The experience on the mountain was, for the disciples, a fog-clearing moment. Jesus was momentarily transformed before them so that they, the chosen ones, could perceive his true status. He is like Moses and Elijah, but yet even greater, for Jesus was immediately set apart from them, a contrast already prepared for by the writer. The point is that the entire narrative does not point forward to the future existence of Jesus, but speaks of his real, although hidden, status on earth. The mountain, the cloud, and the voice do not place the scene in heaven — but point more to its earthly character, since, throughout biblical tradition, these are signs of divine presence on earth. So, too, Jesus was not given new garments, but his earthly ones are said to be glistening. The presence of the disciples throughout the narrative and their real, although confused, role in the event underlines this conclusion.

This act of God, therefore, was like removing the veil that had hidden reality from the disciples so that they were able to glimpse what they had failed to understand up until then. It was a divine revelation regarding Jesus' person. After recognizing him as God's Anointed One, they were then shown the fullness of the mystery of his person: the Anointed Servant of God is also the Beloved son who shares in the glory of God. It is for this reason that they were told, in the stark reality of a divine command, that Jesus must be obeyed.

Thus, the disciples were able to follow because they had had a fog-clearing moment. They had had an immediate experience with Christ which enabled them to keep on going, even when the road was fogged over. They might not have fully understood, but they kept on following because of that one moment when they had had an immediate experience with Christ which enabled them to stay on the road with him. They had to trust in that time when they could see clearly, in order to get through those times when their vision was blurred and uncertain.

Consider the possibility that we are a lot like those first disciples. Like them, we live with misunderstanding. Life is more like a fog than like a clear day when one can see forever. Most of us are able to make it through the fog because we have had certain "mountain-top" experiences with Christ which gave us great certainty about God's presence in the thick darkness. Without these moments of certainty, we would not be able to continue. It is the fog-clearing moments that make it possible for us to navigate through those time when life is more than difficult.

Most of us have had fog-clearing moments. A recent Gallop Poll reported that eighty-five percent of the people interviewed said that they had had a "mystical" experience with God. This is a high percentage! But, when you think about it, there have been those moments in life when we experienced God's presence and purpose in ways that are deep, profound, and real. So great is that certainty that we would stake our lives upon its reality. Perhaps we cannot explain it, but it is real beyond the shadow of a doubt.

Fog-clearing moments have taken different shapes for various types of people. Some people have had mystical experiences. In these mystical experiences, there has been the clear conviction of a living God, as the primary interest of consciousness, and of a personal self capable of communion with God. For others, a fog-clearing moment has come as a flash of insight while worshiping, reading, beholding a work of art, or listening to an anthem which touches the spirit.

A few years ago, I taught a course in United Methodist Policy at Vanderbilt Divinity School. On the first day of class, I asked the students to share a time in their lives when they were especially aware of God's presence. I asked them to talk about a sacred moment in their faith journies which had become for them a mountain-top experience. I was stunned when a majority of the students talked about the death of a significant person as a time when they knew God's presence with great certainty.

Some people have experienced a sign of divine presence while driving away from the hospital with a newborn baby cuddled in a soft blanket. Some have experienced God's revelation while listening to a friend, caring for the poor, or watching a child play basketball.

Phyllis Tickle lives on a farm in West Tennessee. She is the mother of seven. She lives with her physician husband and her three children who are still at home on a large spread near Lucy, Tennessee, just north of Memphis. Experiences on this farm provide the setting for many of her books and articles. Her love for words and her command of language provide the vehicle to convey what she is learning about Christian life and about herself. "I have learned more about what 'Christian' means in a day-to-day 'let's do the dishes again, or change the baby' day than any other thing in the world," said Phyllis Tickle. For Tickle, those day-to-day experiences have become fog-clearing moments. Tickle, like all the rest of us, is moving through the fog of life. We must also trust those moments when there was clarity.

Most of the time, the fog-clearing moments do not come when we set out to look for them. Most of the time, the fog-clearing moments come when we are able to see the divine in the ordinary. Phyllis Tickle said that she never looks for special experiences with God. "Never look for it. Couldn't find it if I did. It overwhelms me. I am attacked by it," said Phyllis.

When those disciples came down the mountain with Jesus, they were still confused about his identity. Was he Elijah? Was he John the Baptizer? Later, the disciples were disappointed because they could not cast the demon out of the epileptic. They were greatly distressed when Jesus said that he would be killed and then raised on the third day. They argued about who would be the greatest in the Kingdom of Heaven. But, they could keep following because there was for them that time on the mountain when they knew beyond a shadow of a doubt.

Like Shrove Tuesday pancake suppers, Transfiguration Sunday immediately precedes Lent. One temptation, especially on Shrove Tuesday, is to stuff ourselves silly with all the sweets that we will be living without for the duration of the coming weeks. Our temptation is to want to stay on the mountain top and to deify the experience. We would rather be alone with the exalted Christ than go down among the people and risk suffering. We, like Peter, have problems with a Christ who suffers. It would be easy to pretend that the exalted Christ, transfigured on the mountain, only appeared to suffer. The Transfiguration functions as the apex of the Gospel.

Who will follow Jesus to Jerusalem? Those who can follow Jesus to Jerusalem are those who have experienced the certainty of his revelation to us. If we do not understand this revelation, it is because we do not see clearly yet. But, just because we do not fully understand it, does not mean that it is any less real. The trick to living the Transfiguration story is to stake our lives on those fog-clearing moments.

About the Author

Dr. Joe E. Pennel, Jr. is the Senior Pastor of the 3,200 member Brentwood United Methodist Church near Nashville, Tennessee. When this book was written, he was the Senior Pastor of Belmont United Methodist Church, a 2,000 member congregation located near Vanderbilt University in Nashville. Former pastorates in Memphis include Frayser Heights, Harris Memorial, and St. Luke.

Dr. Pennel holds a B.A. from Lambuth College and his M.A. and D.Min. from Vanderbilt University. He has continued his interest in theological education by serving as a lecturer in United Methodist Studies at Vanderbilt Divinity School and by chairing the school's Advisory Council.

The author is a member of the World Methodist Council, the Board of Trustees of Martin College and the Board of Friends of General Hospital, Nashville, Tennessee. He preached for the 1984 Cole Lecturers at Vanderbilt Divinity School and has published sermons in *Pulpit Digest* and in the 1985-1988 editions of *Ministers Manual.* Dr. Pennel has been an alternate delegate to the General Conference of the United Methodist Church and a delegate to the Jurisdictional Conference of the United Methodist Church. He chairs the Work Area on Worship for the Tennessee Conference. In addition, Dr. Pennel is a member of the Board of Publications of the United Methodist Church.

Dr. Pennel is the author of *A Connectional Community, The Whisper of Christmas,* and *From Anticipation to Transfiguration.*

www.ingramcontent.com/pod-product-compliance
Lightning Source LLC
LaVergne TN
LVHW021520080426
835509LV00018B/2569